Personal Recollections

of the

Campaigns in
Abyssinia, 1868, and Afghanistan, 1872

Gen. Custer's Last Campaign, 1876
(With Historical Notes and Correspondence)

and the

Hawaiian Rebellion, 1895

By

T. B. WALKER

Honolulu
Advertiser Publishing Co., Ltd.
1931

This book is dedicated to my wife,

Mrs. T. B. Walker

T. B. WALKER

CHAPTER I

1868 ABYSSINIAN CAMPAIGN

Several years of progressive defiance of Great Britain by King Theodore of Abyssinia, who held as prisoners missionaries of England and Germany, caused Great Britain to declare war against Abyssinia. Great Britain sent an expedition, commanded by Sir Robert Napier, against King Theodore. Orders were read out in Chatham giving those who wished to volunteer the privilege to go. My chum, Blanchfire, and myself volunteered to go. We left Chatham the end of December, 1867, and sailed on a troop vessel named Surphrius. We landed at a place called Assobo, just off the Strait of Bab el Mandeb. We marched from Bab el Mandeb to Magdala.

We had our first skirmish at Senafi and our enemy retired quickly to the hills and valleys. We stopped at Senafi three days to rest and then continued the march to Magdala. We camped three miles from the fortification, which was on the heights of Magdala, and the next morning, just before daybreak, advanced up the heights towards Magdala and stormed Magdala's fortified batteries, which only had two cannons, smooth bore. These two cannon shots did not hurt anyone, so therefore no one knew where they had gone to. We used to pass a joke, saying that those two shots are still going. Upon taking the battery one of the guns had been split right across the breech. We always thought that in loading it they double-shot it. We found King Theodore lying by the side of a rice straw stack shot through his head. He either did it himself or one of his followers did it for him. Major Pritchard was shot in the ankle as we were storming the heights and said, "Throw me to one side, lads, and go ahead."

Our infantry rushed through the village and was ordered not to shoot those who would surrender and to brush the women and children aside, as General Napier did not care for bloodshed if it could be avoided.

After a few days we started our homeward march, taking King Theodore's wife and son, and also the English and German missionaries whom King Theodore had taken as prisoners. When we arrived at Senafi, King Theodore's wife died. Upon her death her native attendants, who were ladies in waiting as well as chiefs, asked permission of General Napier if they could take charge of the body. The request was granted.

Major Pritchard, at this time, was doing splendidly, his wound was healing. Lieutenant Morgan went out lion hunting one day; got sunstroke and died. One of the buglers met with the same fate, sunstroke, and he also died. We continued our march from Senafi and reached the shores of the Red Sea without any more obstacles. We had then accomplished about five hundred miles of marching. It was rather tough on account of the trail being mountainous. We laid wires, as well as photographed the country, from the start to Magdala, so we had communication all of the way.

We used the American well-boring machine. It was superior to what we had in England. I was one of the well-boring parties. We were very successful in striking water, and we were always well in advance of the main column, with a strong advance guard to protect us while we were boring. We were paid so much a day for our work, as well as our regimental pay, so we had a nice check to draw when we got back to England. They gave us two months' leave, and gave us permission to wear civilian clothes for two months. Then we returned to duty.

Sir Robert Napier received the title of Lord Napier of Magdala, and Theodore's son was sent to school.

We sailed for England and arrived on the 12th of August, 1868. Later Blanchfire and myself were transferred from the Tenth Company to the Twelfth Company. This company was sent to Fort Candon at Queenstown Harbor, where we were to alter and pull down the old fortification at the entrance and erect new fortifications. These new fortifications, the gun portion, could not be seen. They were to have the Moncrief guns, which, after being loaded in the pit, could be raised and given whatever elevation required for firing. Things went along nicely and in 1872 the ministry heard that Russia was not keeping the treaty which was signed after the Crimean War, in regard to the distance from the gates of Arat, which was supposed to be one hundred miles. Russia had encroached about fifty miles.

Beaconsfield had notified the Amir of Afghanistan of this fact and asked the Amir for permission to survey from the gates of Arat to prove this. The Amir consented, but would not offer any protection. Volunteers were called again to form a survey party to go to Afghanistan. I volunteered and went. This was in 1872. We managed very well on the survey towards the Russian territory because there was a road and Russia was doing considerable trading with Afghanistan. On completing the survey we found that there was only forty-five miles from the gate of Arat to a place called Merv, which was a Russian outpost garrisoned by Cossacks, who treated us very nicely. We spent one week there and then commenced our march back to the gates of Arat. When we were ten miles from the Cossacks' outpost we had considerable trouble with the mountain bandits, who opened fire on us, but no one was hit. We had to keep a sharp lookout both night and day. On the second day after we left Merv they gave us a great deal of trouble, and we in turn did not give them any rest and took every opportunity of knocking them off whenever they showed themselves. We had several very good shots in our party. One was Tom Beckit, who had held the gold rifles in the corps for two years in succession, and a few others who were marksmen. The mountain bandits had only muzzle-loaders, while we had the Snider rifles. We were bothered for two days by them. We were not able to know how many we had killed, but none of our party was hit. We then marched on to the gates of Arat and from there we marched and rode in pull-carts towards Peshawar. It was always thought, by several officers in India, that there were only two ways where an enemy could enter British India, but Lieutenant Andrews had been very inquisitive and had found out that Russia could enter from the Buffet Strait of Afghanistan to the north, which would be about an equal race as to who got to Kabul first.

Afghanistan has an area of 250,000 square miles. The greater part is mountainous. Its plains are, with few exceptions, over 6,000 feet above sea level, with large areas above 7,000 feet. Its principal mountain range is Hindu Kush, 20,000 feet in height, and is traversed by numerous passes, which are of great military and commercial importance. Herat and Kandahar are fertile sections. In most districts crops yield two harvests. Camels and excellent horses are raised. Herat is of great military importance, and a center of carpet manufacture. Kabul is a war munition center. Kandahar is largely engaged in silk manufacture. The population of Afghanistan is about 6,000.

We had gone a little out of our way, but at last got on the right track and entered Peshawar. Had a nice time there for a week and thought that we were going to be sent back to England, but news came of the uprising of mountain tribes in the Punjab district, so we were sent there to join the forces under General Roberts. We had some pretty hard fighting in Simba, Uanda and Uimblls. I got wounded there by a ricochet shot which hit me on the shin bone and knocked a piece of the bone off. I had eight cartridges left and fired them and then gave up. I was attended to about two hours later, and after two weeks I was sent to Delli and was in a hospital there for two weeks. It was said that I would not be fit for marching again, so I was invalided and sent to England, to the Knitley Hospital. My wound got nicely healed up, but was very tender.

CHAPTER II

After one month I was let out of the army with nine pence a day as pension. One week after I was on the scaffold at work in London. Worked for two months there and then went to Sheffield and worked for two weeks, and then I had an opportunity to go to Rotherham to do some work in a coal mine.

Mr. Stubbs was manager. He told me that there was one shaft ready to brick and that there were two others being sunk. This shaft was about fifteen hundred feet deep and it seemed that bricklayers in the vicinity did not care for this kind of work. The first shaft I went to work in had five donkey engines pumping water out to the top. I told Mr. Stubbs that I had never done that kind of work, but that I was willing to work in it. He said they worked six-hour shifts. I got eight shillings a shift. Most of the time I worked two shifts. This was because they wanted the work to get ahead, as it was hard to get bricklayers to work in these shafts.

The sinkers are the men who quarry out the rock to form these shafts. They take out about twenty or twenty-four feet of this rock, which leaves this twenty or twenty-four feet to be built up, and in the building of this brick work in the shafts, what is called crib is put in and buntons. After the pit is finished the runners are connected to the buntons so that these cages which bring up the coal can come up without swaying. They are brought up by a wire rope, and in some pits there are six of these small cars which are hauled up at once and the empty ones let down.

I worked there until the three shafts were finished, which took eight months, and had a little over five hundred pounds in the bank.

I went to London and had a good time there with my mother and sisters, made presents to them and then bought a ticket for New York, as I had made up my mind to go to Australia to start a builders' yard. When I arrived in New York I got in contact with two bricklayers who used to be mechanics when I was an apprentice in the same firm. They were now well-to-do and I stopped three weeks with them. They were in the contracting business and wanted me to stay with them. After stopping three weeks with them I then started off for San Francisco, but only got as far as Wyoming, where I went to work for a man there who had a contract to build the Interocean Hotel. The reason I got off at Cheyenne, Wyoming, was because a man came on the train and asked if there were any bricklayers on board and I replied, "I am a bricklayer." "Well," he said, "if you are a bricklayer, I have about two months' work for you at six dollars a day." This money seemed big to me. I told him about my ticket to San Francisco and of my trunk having gone ahead to San Francisco, which he in turn said, "I will sell your ticket for you and get your trunk back," thus preventing my being much out. I said, "All right," got my things off the train. He got me a room in a boarding house. The proprietor was Charles Kimber, a native of Holland. This happened in October, 1875. The rest about me you will find in 1876, when I volunteered to go in the expedition after Sitting Bull.

Many people from all parts of the United States were fitting out here in Cheyenne for the Black Hills gold excitement. I asked "Wild Bill" if it was any good going there. He said, "No, I know the country; there will be trouble there presently with the Indians," and he added, "maybe later on." I would like to go with the expedition; I would volunteer to go with Custer.

After hearing so many things about the Custer column, I thought it best to go and see for myself. I asked Bill if he would give me a letter of introduction to Captain Tom Custer at Dakota and he did. I went there and had a long talk with Captain Tom Custer and General George Custer. He asked me many questions about the campaigns in Abyssinia and about British India, and then said, "Thank you, Mr. Walker, for the information you have given me; it is very interesting. Now, Mr. Boston Custer might be able to place you in some position, I hope." He gave me a note and told Mr. Reed, his nephew, to take me to Boston. Boston Custer was in his office. Mr. Reed introduced me to him and Captain Calhoun. I gave my letter to Boston. He read it and I explained to him that I would like to go with the expedition in some position where I might be useful. After questioning me he spoke about wages and I told him that I wasn't particular in regard to my salary. "My position is forage master of the Seventh Cavalry and we will need assistance. Give me your address and I will notify you when I know for sure what date we leave."

Now, when I got back to Cheyenne, I told Mr. Hickok the way I was received by these gentlemen and that they sent their kind regards to him. "Well, I am glad you went," he said, "for you know all about it now."

General G. A. Custer

CHAPTER III

CUSTER AND GRANT

Now we will turn to the campaign under General Terry's orders.

When Sheridan and Sherman planned the destruction of Sitting Bull, it was ordered that Custer should be assigned to the command of the Dakota column. It was organized at his post, and was mainly composed of his regiment, and was repeatedly denominated in orders "Custer's Column." The reasons for giving him this post were perfectly simple. Custer had never yet met with a single disaster while in command of an important expedition, and he had been blessed with more success in his Indian expeditions than any other officer in the army. His only rival as an Indian fighter was Crook, and Crook had gained his reputation by an extermination of small, scattered bands of Apaches in Arizona, who were not blessed with a semicircle of Indian agencies in their rear to supply them with Winchester rifles and patent ammunition. Besides this, Crook was getting older, and having been made a brigadier, was not so likely to work as Custer, who was only a lieutenant colonel, thanks to the seniority rule. Brigadier General Terry, the department commander, had never been in the field as an Indian fighter, and felt quite content to leave the Indian laurels to Custer. Terry was a brigadier who owed his sudden elevation to his present rank to the capture of Fort Fisher. Having been a volunteer only, and before that a lawyer, not a West Pointer, Terry found himself in a peculiar position in the army. Had he been a nervous, energetic officer like Custer, the enmity he would have excited among the old seniority officers, especially the graduates, would have been much greater. As it was, while they hated him decisively and had not the same opportunity to spite him, Terry being two steps higher than Custer, only his great sweetness of temper and modesty preserved him from active enmity. Terry trusted Custer implicitly and admired him greatly and it was settled that Custer should lead the Dakota column. Then came a sudden interruption to all these plans, a chain of incidents which ended in a disaster to the nation and in the temporary triumph of Custer's enemies. The facts of this business are so important to the vindication of Custer's character from the attacks of these enemies that the nation of which he was the pride will not seem wasting the space which brings them clearly to light.

While Custer was hard at work preparing for his part of the Sioux Expedition, eager for work and foreseeing a further triumph, he received a telegram from Mr. Helster Clymer, chairman of a certain Congressional Committee, requiring his presence in Washington to give testimony as to some alleged abuses in the War Department at the time Mr. Belknap, who had lately resigned the office of Secretary of War, was under investigation in regard to an alleged sale by him of a post tradership to a person called Marsh. The committee had stumbled on the evidence of this sale by accident, and the Secretary, overwhelmed with shame at the discovery of his upper-post traders now supplying the place of the old settlers, whose office was abolished a few years since. They have the exclusive privilege of trading at the post to which they are appointed, and where the garrison is large the privilege is exceedingly valuable, as much of the pay of soldiers and officers is generally spent in the post trader's store for little luxuries. The post tradership given to Marsh was at Fort Sill, Indian Territory, where ten companies of cavalry were generally stationed, aggregating about six hundred men and forty officers, including staff, etc. The pay of the garrison amounted to about $160,000 a year, and at the ordinary sutler's rates it was pretty certain that at least $100,000 would be spent at the store, with a profit to the post trader at 100 per cent or at least $50,000 per annum.

The defence of the delinquent secretary, so far as it appeared, was that his first wife had, unknown to him, sold her influence with him for the office; that his second wife, sister of the first, had continued the bargain with Marsh after the death of her sister, and that he, Belknap, was perfectly ignorant of the whole matter till shortly before the examination of Marsh, when the shame and misery experienced by him at the exposure of the delinquencies of his two wives was so great as to lead to his giving up the fight in advance. Although this is not the place to enter into the merits or demerits of the Belknap case, which has since been legally settled in his favor, it may be stated that this explanation was believed to be the truth by all those who were personally intimate with the ex-Secretary's career. One of these was President Grant, on whose staff the Secretary had served as General Belknap during the war and who remained his firm friend in his trouble.

The Congressional committee was determined, however, to investigate every act of Belknap's career in regard to frontier posts, and began to call witnesses from all quarters, groping blindly after the facts. The vaguest hearsay evidence was snatched at, and at last some one suggested that General Custer knew something about corruption on the part of the ex-Secretary; he had been heard by some one to say that he had heard something on the subject, and so forth. On this vague information the sapient chairman telegraphed a summons to Custer to come to Washington, and so started a train of circumstances which was to end in the untimely death of the best cavalry chief on the American continent. Custer was much disturbed. He telegraphed at once to Terry to know what he should do, stating that his own information was only hearsay and devoid of value to the case, and asking whether an order was not necessary. He made these inquiries of Terry, knowing that his general had been bred a lawyer. At the same time, showing his scrupulous sense of justice, he asked whether he was not bound to go, and tell what little he knew and how he knew it. In the same telegram, showing his peculiarly sensitive honor, he asks for a court of inquiry on himself in regard to his own conduct towards a discontented officer of his regiment, concerning a transfer from one company to another, in which the officer complained that injustice had been done him. Terry's answer to this telegram was as follows:

Hdqrs. Dept. of Dakota, St. Paul, Minn., March 16, 1876.
To Lieut. Col. Custer, Fort Lincoln, Dakota:

Despatch received. You need no order beyond the summons of the committee. I am sorry to have you go, for I fear it will delay our movements. I should suppose that if your testimony is not as to the facts themselves, and will only point out the witnesses from whom the committee can get the facts, your information might be communicated by letter or telegraph, and that being done, you might ask to be relieved from personal attention without exposing yourself to misconstruction. However, you must use your own judgment.

In regard to the other matter, I don't think that you need a court of inquiry. Your statement to me vindicated you in my eyes: a repetition to General Sheridan would doubtless vindicate you in his. A court could not be convened until after the summer campaign is over. Your services are indispensable, and no thought of a transfer can be entertained.

TERRY, Comd'g. Dept.

Custer took Terry's advice and telegraphed to Clymer as follows:

Fort Lincoln, Dakota, March 16, 1876.
Hon. Helster Clymer:

While I hold myself in readiness to obey the summons of your committee, I telegraph to state that I am engaged upon an important expedition, intended to operate against the hostile Indians, and I expect to take the field early in April. My presence here is deemed very necessary. In view of this, would it not be satisfactory for you to forward to me such questions as may be necessary, allowing me to return my replies by mail?

GEO. A. CUSTER.

Clymer, proud of his power to see through a millstone much further than anyone else, would not be denied, and made Custer come on, besides putting him through a cross-examination that lasted two days and compelling him to tell not only all he knew, but all he did not know into the bargain. After a month's torture of Custer, he finally found out that the latter had written him an honest letter, and that the committee might better have left him in Fort Lincoln.

To only one fact was Custer able to testify of his own knowledge. This was that, on one occasion, the contractor at Fort Lincoln had turned over to him a large quantity of grain in sacks which had borne the Indian brand, and which he suspected had been stolen from the Indian Department, as part of the gigantic system of fraud by which the Indian Ring played into the hands of army contractors. At the time this grain was issued to Custer he refused to receive it, and telegraphed to Department Headquarters on the subject, expressing his suspicions. In due time, his communication having been forwarded through regular channels, he received a positive order to take the grain. This order, he stated to the committee, he believed to have come down from the Secretary of War. This evidence, while avowedly only on information and belief, was regarded by Clymer as implicating the Secretary in some fresh fraud, and on the face of things there was ample ground for Custer's honest suspicions of the whole business. It turned out afterwards that Custer was mistaken as to the origin of the peremptory order. It really came from Terry alone, on the latter's responsibility. We shall see later how perfectly frank Custer was in the matter and how ready publicly to retract his error.

Much has been said by strong political partisans as to this last public action of Custer. By those who were ardent supporters of the ex-Secretary, and especially of his avowed friend, President Grant, the indirect and hearsay testimony which was all that Custer could give, was contrasted with the previous parade of its promised value made by the committee, and especially by the partisan newspapers on the side of the committee. Custer was called a "swift witness," a "retailer of gossip," and accused of intriguing for his summons in order to escape frontier duty. Much of this abuse might be now passed over on the score of partisan excitement, were it not that the writer of Custer's biography feels himself bound by a sense of duty to probe the truth to the very bottom.

As regards the Belknap case, it is certain that Custer's evidence was wholly immaterial. His only item of personal knowledge adverse to the Secretary was founded on an honest mistake, which he was swift to acknowledge when it was pointed out to him. As a witness of the prosecution, he should never have been called.

Who called him?

Helster Clymer and that ingenious committee which so studiously mismanaged the Belknap case, were the real parties to blame. Custer had telegraphed to Clymer, begging to be excused from attendance at Washington, as an important expedition was about to take the field, in which his presence was necessary. He earnestly begged to be left at his post, but his request was denied. Clymer was bound to have him in Washington for political effect, just as Johnson in old times had been determined to have Custer's name associated with his in "swinging around the circle." In both cases the only party injured was the honest, unsuspecting soldier. The more Clymer questioned him, the more ludicrous was his failure to extract anything but the truth. For this truth Custer has been blamed by his enemies, when the real party to blame was the officious chairman who persisted in calling him. On Clymer's shoulders, moreover, rests the responsibility of deferring Custer's departure after Sitting Bull a whole month. Had he gone in April, before the Indians had gathered in force, Custer might be alive now.

One person in the United States, however, would not believe in Custer's unwillingness to testify. Instead of this, he took Custer's presence and testimony in Washington as a personal affront to himself. This person was President Grant.

President Grant was once General Grant. As General Grant he was chiefly distinguished for one virtue, an indomitable resolution and obstinacy in following whatever plan he had resolved on, an iron determination to pursue it at whatever cost. This quality of determination in war had finally conducted him to success, because as a general his power was absolute. As the executive of a republic, it brought him hatred and ill-will, for the successful head of a republic must be an eloquent and persuasive man, who can win others to his side by flattery and who knows how to yield outwardly, while gaining his ends by craft and subtlety.

Another virtue possessed by General Grant was that of faithfulness to his friends, and this virtue also tended to his success in war, while in peace it operated in exactly the opposite direction. Had it been accompanied by good judgment in the choice of friends, it might not have been so disastrous, but, unluckily, Grant seems from the first to have fallen into the hands of very questionable friends, who would have fleeced him had he been a rich man, who were accused of fleecing the nation under his protection, he being a high officer.

The efforts of the Clymer committee and the House during the Belknap investigation had undoubtedly been directed towards the injury of Grant and his friends, who formed what was known under the general term of "the Administration"; and the animus of the whole attack was so evident, the persistency of the efforts to find something on which to hang more impeachments so untiring, that they had excited the bitterest indignation in Grant himself. His very virtues, pride, firmness, faithful friendship, conviction of honesty, tended to embitter his animosity against all connected with the attack on "his Administration." He looked on them as mortal enemies, and never forgave them. Amongst these he now counted Custer. He never paused to inquire whether the latter was a willing witness, whether his testimony was dragged out of him or not; he made up his mind that Custer had turned against him in his period of trial, and he became bitterly and inexorably incensed against him personally. Custer heard of this, through private sources, and knew that the President's impression as to his own testimony was quite unfounded. As soon, therefore, as he was released from his attendance at the committee, he called at the White House to pay his respects to the President, hoping by a frank personal statement to disabuse his mind of the mistake. For the first time in his life, Custer found himself treated with ignominy, compelled to wait in the anteroom for hours, to see other persons getting audiences before him, while he himself was left perfectly unnoticed, although his card was sent in from the first. Three times he called at the White House, and on neither occasion was he even noticed. These visits were made at various times during his sojourn at Washington, while he was daily expecting his release and return to Dakota. He had left the fort expecting to be gone ten days at furthest; he had now been detained at Washington for over a month, unable to go anywhere, uncertain of his movements from day to day. He was only able to take one hurried trip to New York on one occasion to have a little business talk with his publishers about his "War Memoirs," which he had commenced during the past winter at Fort Lincoln. This hurried visit was the occasion of the last glimpse of Custer caught by the writer of this biography, while in the editorial rooms of the "Galaxy." Custer looked worn and thin and somewhat worried, his hair cut short, a great change from the debonair cavalier of the Waynesboro' fight. His manner conveyed the impression of a nervous man with his nerves all on edge, in a state of constant repressed impatience. He had left his wife behind at Fort Lincoln, and knew that every day brought the season of active operations nearer, while he was away. No wonder he looked worried. At last he was released from his attendance, May 1st, and went to the White House, with a last, almost despairing effort, to get an audience from Grant and to explain his action. Once more he was compelled to submit to the slight of being kept waiting in the anteroom among the President's lackeys. Time was going on; his detention by the official summons was over, and he knew that his duty imperatively called him back to Fort Lincoln, that very day. He sat down and wrote the following note, which he sent in:

To His Excellency, the President:

Today for the third time I have sought an interview with the President—not to solicit a favor, except to be granted a brief hearing—but to remove from his mind certain unjust impressions concerning myself, which I have reason to believe are entertained against me. I desire this opportunity simply as a matter of justice, and I regret that the President has declined to give me an opportunity to submit to him a brief statement, which justice to him, as well as to me, demanded.

Respectfully submitted,

G. A. Custer,
Lt. Col. Seventh Cavalry,
Bvt. Maj. Gen. U. S. Army.

This letter was sent in to and read by the President. During the last visit, as we are credibly informed, General Ingalls, then acting Quartermaster General, found Custer in the anteroom and went in to see the President. Ingalls was a good and just man, and a friend of both. He asked the President if he knew that Custer was outside, waiting. The President did—he did not wish to see him. Then, Ingalls urged, he should at least spare Custer the indignity of waiting outside, and send him a message to save his time—that so much was due to Custer's past services at least. Then the President sent out word that he refused to see Colonel Custer, and Custer sat down and wrote his quiet, manly letter, honest and proud, sad and dignified, like himself in every word. It was useless. Grant refused to see him.

Custer had no longer any pretext for staying in Washington. He had already been to call on the General of the army, and found that Sherman was away in New York, but was expected back in the evening. He went off and secured his passage on the night train, calling on Inspector General Marcy and Adjutant General Townsend on the way. Adjutant General Marcy had wished Custer, on the way back to Dakota, to perform some duty in Detroit which would delay him, but hearing from Custer of the urgency of his haste, on account of the lateness of the season, and of the necessity of his immediate presence at Fort Lincoln, gave him the following letter:

War Department, Inspector General's Office,
Washington, D. C., May 1st, 1876.

LIEUT. COL. G. A. CUSTER, U. S. Army:

Colonel:—Understanding that the general of the army desires you to proceed directly to your station, the service which I recommended you to perform in Detroit, Michigan, can be executed by another officer. And in the absence of the general you have my consent to omit stopping at Detroit for the purpose specified in the Adjutant General's letter to you.

Very respectfully, your obedient servant,

R. B. MARCY, Inspector General.

Custer made a last call at Sherman's office. The General was not back from New York, and his length of stay was still uncertain. Custer took the train and was soon whirling away toward Chicago. The next day, May 2d, General Sheridan was awakened from his slumbers by the following extraordinary telegram:

Washington, D. C., May 2d, 1876.

GENERAL P. H. SHERIDAN, Chicago, Illinois:

I am this moment advised that General Custer started last night for Saint Paul and Fort Abraham Lincoln. He was not justified in leaving without seeing the President or myself. Please intercept him at Chicago or Saint Paul and order him to halt and await further orders. Meanwhile, let the Expedition from Fort Lincoln proceed without him.

(Signed) W. T. SHERMAN, General.

It was the hand of Sherman, but the head of Grant. The grim, implacable animosity of the President was aroused. Custer's testimony had made him the President's foe. Right or wrong, Grant was determined to punish him, and there was but one way to do it—deprive him of the command of the expedition, and so humiliate him. No one knew better than Grant that if Custer went in command of the Dakota column he was certain to return victorious, with fresh laurels. That pill was too bitter for the President to swallow. All that Sheridan could do, in the face of such a positive order, was to obey it. An officer was sent to the station and Custer was stopped on the 4th of May by the following letter:

Headquarters Military Div. of the Missouri,
Chicago, Ill., May 4th, 1876.

LIEUTENANT-COL. G. A. CUSTER, Seventh U. S. Cavalry,
  Chicago, Ill.:

Sir:—Agreeable to instructions contained in the enclosed copy of a telegraphic dispatch from the general of the army, of the 2d instant, the Lieutenant-General commanding the division directs you to remain in Chicago until the receipt of further orders from superior authority, to be furnished you through these headquartes.

Very respectfully, your obedient servant,

R. C. DRUM, Assistant Adjutant General.

There was nothing to it but to obey. Custer drove in haste to Sheridan's headquarters and found him as friendly as ever. Sheridan knew no more of the cause of the order than did Custer himself, and told him so. He had no objection to Custer's telegraphing direct to Sherman for an explanation, and the astonished officer at once sent off the following dispatch:

Chicago, Ill.

GENERAL W. T. SHERMAN, Washington, D. C.:

I have seen your despatch to General Sheridan directing me to await orders here, and am at a loss to understand that portion referring to my departure from Washington without seeing you or the President, as I called at the White House at 10 o'clock A. M. Monday, sent my card to the President, and, with the exception of a few minutes' absence at the War Department, I remained at the White House waiting an audience with the President until 3 P. M., when he sent word that he would not see me. I called at your office about 2 P. M., but was informed by Colonel McCook you had not returned from New York, but were expected in the evening. I called at your hotel at 4 P. M. and about 6 P. M., but was informed by the clerk that you had not returned from New York. I then requested Colonel McCook to inform you of the substance of the above dispatch, and also that I was to leave at 7 that evening to report to my command.

While at the War Department that day I also reported the fact of my proposed departure to the Adjutant General and to the Inspector General of the army, and obtained from them written and verbal authority to proceed to my command without visiting Detroit, as previously ordered to do. At my last interview with you, I informed you that I would leave Washington Monday night to join my command, and you, in conversation replied that "that was the best thing I could do." Besides, you frequently, during my stay in Washington, called my attention to the necessity for my leaving as soon as possible. I telegraph you direct, with the permission of the Lieutenant General.

G. A. CUSTER, Brevet Major General.

Later in the day he sent this further telegram:

Chicago, May 4, 1876, 2:30 P. M.
GEN. W. T. SHERMAN, Washington, D. C.:

I desire to further call your attention to your statement to me, in your office, that I should go in command of my regiment.

Also to your reply when I inquired if the President or other parties had any charges to make against me. In leaving Washington, I had every reason to believe I was acting in strict accordance with your suggestions and wishes. I ask you as General of the army to do me justice in this matter.

G. A. CUSTER.

No answer came to these despatches, and Custer well knew the reason. It was not Sherman who was thus putting him to torture, but some one behind Sherman who was able to command him. Grant was resolved to humiliate Custer, no matter at what cost. He was stolidly determined to have his own way. As a last resort, Custer telegraphed a third time in the evening.

GENERAL W. T. SHERMAN, Washington, D. C.:

After you read my despatch of today, I would be glad if my detention could be authorized at Fort Lincoln, where my family is, instead of at this point.

G. A. CUSTER, Bvt. Major General.

Not a word in answer to all this. Custer had committed no crime; there were no charges against him. He had done nothing but obey orders all through, but it was necessary he should be punished, as the President could punish no one else. In this Grant showed great knowledge of human nature. No doubt he would have liked immediately to punish every officer who had testified against his "administration," but he had no means by which to do it. No one else of the witnesses was in command of an expedition, no one was a successful Indian fighter, no one else was a high-strung, nervous cavalier, sensitive to slight. Custer was the only man. It was so easy to punish him, by the simplest means; the reason assigned was so plausible. Grant knew that the torture lay in the first humiliation, the minor details were of little consequence. After all, the President, while a bitter foe, was not a cruel one. He had no objection to letting Custer see his family. So it appears by the following despatch:

Chicago, May 5th.

Brigadier General A. H. Terry, St. Paul, Minn.:

The Lieutenant General directs me to transmit for your information and guidance the following telegram from the General of the Army:

"Have received your dispatch of today, announcing General Custer's arrival. Have just come from the President, who orders that General Custer be allowed to rejoin his post, to remain there on duty, but not to accompany the expedition supposed to be on the point of starting against the hostile Indians under General Terry.

(Signed)   "W. T. Sherman, General."

Please acknowledge receipt.

(Signed)   R. C. Drum, A. A. G.,
Hdqrs. Dept. of Dakota,

St. Paul, May 8th, 1876.

Official copy respectfully furnished for the information of Lieutenant Colonel Custer.

Geo. Ruggles, Asst. Adj. Gen.

It appears clearly from the next message that Sherman was not inimical to Custer, for he telegraphed to him kindly enough. Immediately following Sherman's telegram will be found one from Custer, illustrating the frankness and completeness with which he always acknowledged his errors. It is the one we have before referred to, as connected with the matter of the grain frauds. Sheridan's telegram is as follows:

Washington, D. C.

GEN. G. A. CUSTER, Chicago, Ill.:

Before receipt of yours, had sent orders to General Sheridan to permit you to go to Abe Lincoln on duty, but the President adheres to his conclusion that you are not to go on the expedition.

W. T. SHERMAN, General.

The other telegram is as follows:

Saint Paul, May 6th, 1876.

To HON. HELSTER CLYMER, Washington, D. C.:

General Terry, commanding the Department of Dakota, informs me that the report I forwarded from Fort Lincoln, regarding certain corn delivered at that post, for the use of the army, in Indian sacks, was received at his headquarters in the city, and after due investigation was acted upon finally by his authority; and that it was he and not the late Secretary of War, who sent the order to Fort Lincoln, directing that, under certain instructions intended to protect the government, the corn in question should be received. The receipt of the order was reported to me, and at the same time I derived the impression that the order emanated from the War Department. As I would not knowingly do injustice to any individual, I ask that this telegram may be appended to and made part of my testimony before your committee.

G. A. CUSTER.

Then Custer found himself, May 6, in St. Paul, and condemned by the President's order to remain behind and see his comrades go to war. How bitterly it must have recalled to him his equally unjust detention, eight years before, at Fort Leavenworth, and the disasters to the nation which had followed his punishment. That punishment led to the Phil Kearny massacre and Forsyth's disastrous siege on the island. It shows how free from vulgar ambition and how pure was Custer's patriotism, that he, the proud soldier, publicly insulted and humiliated without the pretence of a fault on his part, should have written such a letter as this, which follows. The last words we commend to the nation that loves him. We also commend Terry's letter of transmittal.

Headquarters Department of Dakota,
Saint Paul, Minn., May 6th, 1876.

ADJUTANT GENERAL, Division of Missouri, Chicago:

I forward the following:

To His Excellency, the President, through Military Channels:

I have seen your order, transmitted through the general of the army, directing that I be not permitted to accompany the expedition about to move against hostile Indians. As my entire regiment forms a part of the proposed expedition, and as I am the senior officer of the regiment on duty in this department, I respectfully but most earnestly request that while not allowed to go in command of the expedition, I may be permitted to serve with my regiment in the field.

I appeal to you as a soldier to spare me the humiliation of seeing my regiment march to meet the enemy and I not to share its dangers.

(Signed) G. A. CUSTER,
Bvt. Maj. Genl. U. S. Army.

In forwarding the above, I wish to say expressly, that I have no desire whatever to question the orders of the President, or of my military superiors. Whether Lieut. Col. Custer shall be permitted to accompany my column or not, I shall go in command of it.

I do not know the reasons upon which the orders already given rest; but if those reasons do not forbid it, Lieut. Col. Custer's services would be very valuable with his command.

(Signed) TERRY, Commanding Department.

The appearance of General Custer before the investigating committee at Washington and the effect of his testimony upon the public mind are already familiar to the reader. The fact came upon his most intimate friends unannounced, and the unfavorable comments of the party press upon his evidence and his character caused the greatest surprise to those who knew him best. The most reserved and reticent of men had suddenly become politically conspicuous, and calumny was busy with that hitherto spotless name. The political temper of the time had undoubtedly much to do with the effect produced by his testimony. The strife of party, and the bitterness with which men of opposite opinions assailed each other; the influence upon the approaching election of the investigation then going forward; the reputation for truth and candor never denied to General Custer, combined to make the attacks upon him unusually severe. He had never obtruded his political sentiments, but they were known to his friends and were never disowned. He could not have sought the unenviable position in which he found himself; he had endeavored by every honorable means to escape from it, but in vain. The effect upon his nature of the abuse suddenly heaped upon him may be measured by the desire he had always evinced to escape public observation, except in the line of his duty; and this was, undoubtedly, one of the saddest eras of his life. The esteem of his countrymen, earned by years of hard service and dearly prized, seemed in an instant to be taken from him. His report upon the evils of the post-trading system had been forwarded to the head of his department long before; his acquaintance with those evils was known to many; not to have answered frankly the questions of the committee would have exposed him to self-contempt. How easily could he have trimmed his sail to the popular breeze, and floated into the smooth waters of political favor. The promotion which his valor had earned; which was due to his merit; which had been bestowed upon his inferiors, lay within his grasp, but the sacrifice was one from which his proud soul revolted. The perfect integrity of his character should never be sullied, to purchase that preferment which had been denied to his public services, and which was in every way due him. He could honestly exclaim, "It is better to be right than to hold the most exalted rank." That he was wounded none who knew him can doubt. In the midst of those exposures which tarnished the reputation of so many brother officers he had happily escaped. At his post upon the distant frontier, occupied with the duties which he loved, surrounded by a small band who regarded their young commander with veneration, he might well feel happy in his escape from that political whirlpool which engulphed so many of his friends, and which swallowed up reputations gained in hard-fought fields. Now, against his will, called peremptorily from the organization of his command, he found himself helplessly drawn into the current, publicly condemned for speaking that which he knew to be true, commented upon by enemies in the coarsest terms, the target of political rancor. The depth of his humiliation was reached, when, upon leaving the capital, he waited for hours at the door of the President, and was at last turned away with studied contempt. The effect of these slights upon his proud and sensitive heart may be imagined. Upheld as he was by the conscience which whispered that he had done his duty, he must still have suffered much in concealing his sorrow from the world; though he scorned to complain, as he would have scorned to bend before the calumny of his enemies.

Our last meeting, which took place at the close of his first visit to Washington, was yet full of happiness. Rallied upon his political relations, he sunnily threw aside his chagrin and seemed indifferent to all but the approaching separation, anxious only that our plan for the next winter should not fail. No premonition of danger clouded our parting. The thought that he was going into action, into certain peril, did not make me fearful. He was so associated with success, had escaped from so many dangers, his long future career was so hopeful, that he seemed invincible. He predicted a severe campaign, but was not doubtful of the result. His plans were well laid, his command efficient, and he joyfully obeyed the summons to return to his duty, happy to escape from the scene where truth was repaid with calumny.

The delay in Chicago; the deprivation of command which overtook him there by order of the President; all these anxious days passed while awaiting the orders of his superiors, were undeserved cruelties. The influences which at length ended his suspense and gave him a subordinate place in the expedition planned by himself, have been explained elsewhere. The disgrace of being supplanted by an inferior in rank or an envious rival was averted, and thus much of the bitterness of his position softened. If he could have chosen his successor, he could not have been better pleased than with the appointment of General Terry. Under him he declared he would go with the command, if obliged to serve as a common soldier. By the tender consideration and courtesy of that gallant officer Custer was permitted to recover that confidence in himself of which his unmerited trials must have well-nigh robbed him. With the delicacy of a gentleman, the appreciation of a kindred soul, Terry restored him to the command which was his due, in fact, if not in appearance, and brought to his aid the advice and experience of the young cavalier whose counsel would be invaluable, whose valor and foresight would be a support, and to whose sword the service would so soon be indebted for its defence. Those who knew General Custer best can well understand how he valued such a privilege. To have been left behind would have been worse than death, when his gallant Seventh and so many of his old comrades were in the field. As he rode out of Fort Lincoln for the last time, he was as full of glee as a child; his duty lay before him, his glory, of which no enemy could rob him. That the wishes of the nation, which followed that gallant band and looked hopefully forward to its movements as a final solution of the Indian question, dwelt with the greatest confidence upon the frontier experience of General Custer, will scarcely be denied. In every campaign he had been victorious, and the wiles and stratagems of the foe were familiar to him. Calumny and envy must be silent before the intrepid heroism of that immortal band as they rode into the "jaws of death," where perished not only the noble Custer and his adoring followers, but also the hope of a nation, the shield of a devoted family.

Glancing back over these pages, how poor and unworthy seems the picture I would paint. Compared with the image engraved upon the heart, this transcript is cold and artificial. When the smoke of the battle has passed away, when envy and cowardice have been consigned to their merited oblivion, some truer likeness shall be made of him who was the bravest of the brave. His career may be thus briefly given: He was born in obscurity; he rose to eminence; denied social advantages in his youth, his untiring industry supplied them; the obstacles to his advancement became the stepping-stones to his fortunes, free to choose for good or evil, he chose rightly; truth was his striking characteristic; he was fitted to command, for he had learned to obey; his acts found their severest critic in his own breast; he was a good son, a good brother, a good and affectionate husband, a Christian soldier, a steadfast friend. Entering the army, a cadet in early youth, he became a General while still on the threshold of manhood; with ability undenied, with valor proved on many a hard-fought field, he acquired the affection of the nation; and he died in action at the age of 37; died as he would have wished to die; no lingering disease preying upon that iron frame. At the head of his command, the messenger of death awaited him; from the field of battle where he had so often "directed the storm," his gallant spirit took its flight. Cut off from aid; abandoned in the midst of incredible odds; waving aloft the sabre which had won him victory so often; the pride and glory of his comrades, the noble Custer fell: bequeathing to the nation his sword; to his comrades his example; to his friends a memory; and to his beloved one a Hero's name.

It will be seen that Terry is cautious as to expressing an opinion, being restrained from speaking out by official reticence. He could not say to his superior officer, whether he thought it or not: "Look here; this is a scandalous shame. Custer has done nothing wrong, he has only obeyed the law and told the truth; and the President is taking a mean and cowardly advantage of his power to punish Custer indirectly, because he dare not do it directly." The old adroitness of the lawyer appears in all of Terry's conduct. He makes no enemies; even the old West Pointers, over whose heads Fort Fisher had jumped him, could not find it in their hearts to hate him.

But the opposition papers were not so mealy-mouthed. All over the land they teemed with double-leaded articles on "Grant's tyranny" and "Custer's degradation," and took the quarrel up, not because they cared for Custer, but because they could make political capital out of it. All the foul vultures of politics flocked to see the battle, expecting a feast at its conclusion. The "Administration" papers were thus in a manner forced into the fight, and into an attitude of antagonism to Custer, which has pursued him beyond his grave. This was unfortunate enough, and it is to be hoped that it will go no further. I have written in this chapter a plain statement of facts, and introduced copies of the original documents, on purpose to show that Custer's action in the whole of this matter was entirely unpolitical, and in the earnest hope that it may prevent his memory from being made the subject of a partisan fight. No man was ever more thoroughly an honest soldier and less of a politician than Custer, and no man has suffered more from the efforts of those vampires of life, the politicians, to make use of him in their quarrels.

Two men were to blame for all the trouble: meddling, officious Helster Clymer, who insisted on making Custer come to Washington; obstinate, implacable Grant—the man, not the President—who would not listen to a word, and who was actually willing to imperil the whole fate of the Sioux campaign and to permit hundreds of lives to be lost, to gain his revenge on Custer. The question has nothing to do with one party or the other, but the responsibility of all that follows rests personally on these two men—the busy-body and the implacable tyrant. One was willing to imperil a nation to serve his faction, the other was ready to forget his office, to prostitute his position, to sacrifice a hecatomb of innocent lives, to gratify his private revenge. From the consequences of that act he cannot escape.

Grant was satisfied with his first disgrace of Custer, or dared not face the criticism which would have greeted the announcement of the fact that the President of the United States was willing to imperil the success of an important expedition to gratify his private revenge. That was going a step too far: so Grant yielded to Custer's petition so far as to let him go as a subordinate, in the expedition which Grant well knew in his heart that Custer alone was fit to command.

The papers said this openly, both opposition and independents, whereupon the administration papers felt themselves compelled to print alleged utterances of General Sherman to the effect that there were "plenty of officers in the army just as capable as Custer." Here again the officious meddling of Custer's injudicious friends only embittered his single real enemy, Grant, and compelled Sherman, as an official person, to appear hostile to Custer. Possibly the general of the army did say there were plenty of officers fit to take Custer's place, but he knew well enough that there was not one, for it was now May 7th, and the operations of every other officer had so far been marked by want of energy all through, especially in the fiasco of the Powder River fight. The fact was, and Sherman, Grant and Sheridan knew it, none better, that no one could replace Custer's peculiar qualities. "Custer," said Sheridan at Fort Leavenworth, seven years before, "you are the only man that never failed me."

Write those words in gold on his monument. None could wish a prouder epitaph.

CHAPTER IV

Well, it broke all my plans with Mr. Boston Custer, so I went to Fort Russell where the Third Cavalry lay. They were taking a few men as drivers, and I had made up my mind to go, and I told the quartermaster about Boston Custer's promise and my experience in warfare. "Are you an American citizen," he said. "No, I have only been in America four months." The quartermaster said, "Well, I will let you know tomorrow." In the morning I went and it was all right, not as a scout, but as a rigger, knotting and splicing.

Now this column was supposed to be a part of the Crook Column which was to follow later. Reynolds started this column

---

NOTE.—Since this chapter was printed and stereotyped, the author has received information from the publishers of the Galaxy that tends further to disprove the accusation that Custer was willing to go to Washington before the committee. In conversation with members of the firm, while on his way to Washington, Custer distinctly stated that he knew nothing of his own knowledge as to the Belknap or other cases that could be of the slightest value to the committee. He displayed the greatest anxiety to be back at his post, and the peremptory summons of the committee was a great disappointment to him. As he expressed it, he had "begged of the committee to allow him to remain at Fort Lincoln, where he was so busy preparing the expedition of which he had been promised the command."

Mrs. Custer, who of all persons is most capable of judging of her husband's wishes, has also most positively assured the author that it was with the greatest unwillingness that Custer departed from Fort Lincoln, and with the fear before his eyes that it would end in disaster to the expedition.

on the 1st of March, 1876, from Fort Fetterman, and it struck off to the Powder River. The column consisted of about eight hundred men of cavalry and infantry and one month's supplies on pack mules and in wagons and was commanded by brevet Major-General Reynolds, Third Cavalry.

We left the wagon train on the 17th inst., with orders to make for Lodgepole. We then scouted the Tongue and Rosebud Rivers until satisfied that there were no Indians upon them, then marching toward the Powder River. Then General Reynolds, with part of the command, went forward leading to the village of Crazy Horse, near the mouth of the Little Powder River. This he attacked and destroyed on the 17th instant, finding it a perfect magazine of ammunition, of war material and general supplies. Crazy Horse had with him the Cheyennes and some of the Minneconjous. In all, one-half of the Indians' reservation. Every evidence we found to prove these Indians in partnership with Red Cloud and Spotted Tail Agencies and that the proceeds of their raids upon the settlements had been taken to those agencies and supplies brought out in return.

Now Crook and staff officers wondered how it could have been done, but it was plain that the Indians had been too cunning for the whole outfit. Now about the Powder River fight, before reaching the final precipices which overlooked the river bed, we discovered a village of one hundred lodges lay in the valley at the foot of the bluffs. It was about eight o'clock, the sun shone brightly, for which we were all glad, for the night had been very cold. Now the column was halted, and Noyes' battalion, second cavalry was ordered up to the front. It consisted of Company "I," second cavalry, Captain Noyes, and Company "K," second cavalry, Captain Eagen. Now this battalion was ordered to descend to the valley. I was ordered to report to Captain Eagen and help get the horses down through the gorges, and while Captain Eagen charged the camp, Captain Noyes was to cut out the herd of horses that could be seen in the valley feeding and drive it up the river. Moore's battalion, consisting of Company "F," Third Cavalry and Company "E," Second Cavalry, was ordered to dismount and go along the ridge to a position covering the side of the village, opposite that which Captain Eagen was to charge. Captain Mill's battalion was ordered to follow Eagen, dismount, and support him in the engagement which might follow the charge. Now we began the descent of the mountain. Now we were all stuck, the sides of the mountain were almost perpendicular, and it seemed almost impassable. I have seen places in India and Abyssinia, but this is the worst. Hours were occupied in getting the horses of the charging column down those rough sides of the mountains, and when a point was reached where the men could mount their horses and go toward the village in the valley, Moore's battalion had not been able to gain its position on the eastern side along the edges of the mountain. Indians could be seen driving their horses to the river, but nothing indicated that they knew of our approach. Just about ten o'clock Captain Eagen rounded the point of the mountain nearest the river, and now in walk and then in a rapid trot went straight for the village. We went in column of twos, now about one hundred and fifty yards from the village. Command, "Left front into line," and with a yell off we went into the encampment. Captain Noyes in the meantime had started the herd up the river. Now the Indians sprang up and started a rapid fire on all sides. Eagan charged through the village three times before Moore's and Mills' battalions got within supporting distance, and things were getting hot; formed line under cover of some high willows at the south side of the camp and poured in rapid volleys upon the Indians, who thought we only had one company, but when the other battalions appeared, advancing as skirmishers, and pouring in a fire of musketry, they ran from all sides and got in the rocks on the sides of the mountain. Now there were over one hundred lodges and immense quantities of robes and fresh meat, and besides, over seven hundred head of horse we had in our possession. Now firing from the side of the mountain, the Indians began in rapid fire from their hiding place. The fire was not very effective. I think they had the same trouble with their Winchester rifles as our men had had, the wire getting so hot it would not throw the shell out. The fire seemed to cease occasionally. It seemed to be very bad markmanship on both sides. Now remember, Reynolds gave orders to set fire to the camp and work of destruction was going on. Now the Indians made a determined attack on the troops about noon, to try and regain possession of the camp. Captain Mills, who had charge of the skirmish line, asked for more men. These were sent promptly, so the attack was quickly and well repulsed, the Indians making for the mountainsides again. Now the work of destruction was finished and we had taken not a thing from the camp—only the horses—of all the good things there were in the camp which we wanted so badly. There were plenty of troops to have kept the Indians clear of the camp while the things we badly wanted could have been taken, but Reynolds gave the order to withdraw all of the troops, and the whole command got out rapidly and made for the river and he kept us going for twenty miles, to a place called

Lodgepole Creek, and there we went into camp, after two days and one night of continual marching.

It was now plain that Reynolds had cold feet and it was nightfall and Moore's and Eagen's companies, Second Cavalry, were the rear guard and assisted Major Stanton and the scouts in bringing up the herd of horses. A good many were shot on the road, and those left reached camp about nine o'clock p. m. It was a bitter cold night and most of the troups had been in the saddle for thirty-six hours, all but four or five hours of which was fighting on foot. Both officers and men were tired out. The horses had had no grazing and showed signs of complete exhaustion when we got to Lodgepole, and what made things bad for us all was that four companies had not arrived. No one had any supper or blankets, so you can imagine what the night was to officers and men and horses. We all knew where the fault was, but not a murmur was heard.

I received a wound in my neck, but I could get around. Some of the wounded lay upon the snow all night, and it was very cold. In the morning we learned that four dead men had been left behind to be mutilated by the Indians. These men could have been taken along easily, but were not, which caused a great deal of dissatisfaction among the troops.

Saturday, at noon, the remainder of the command arrived. In the meantime a portion of the horses had strayed into the ravines and into the hands of the Indians again.

It is improper to close this sketch of the engagement without referring more particularly to those causes which prevented its complete success. First among these was the failure of Captain Moore's battalion to reach the position assigned it in the rear of the village, or a point covering the rear, before the charge was made by Captain Eagen. This failure allowed the Indians to make good their escape to the sides of the mountains overlooking the valley and from which they poured in a galling fire upon our troops. Moore's battalion was a strong one in number and needed only to march to the front, where it could be effective to do good service. When it was discovered that the battalion would not be at the place assigned it, and that its commander did not apparently intend to put it there, Major Stanton and Lieut. Sibley with five men left him and went on, taking up the position which the battalion should have occupied and gave the flying Indians the best fire they could, but they were too few to prevent the escape of the Indians. This was the first serious blunder. The next was that after the herd of ponies, over seven hundred, had been captured and driven twenty miles from the scene of action, and turned

MAJOR STANTON (SATANTA)

over to General Reynolds, commanding the troops, he did not place a guard around them, so the Indians got most of their ponies back. But what about the large quantity of buffalo robes, blankets and food, which General Crook had directed, in case of capture, to be brought out for the use of the troops, who were on half rations of fresh meat? This was not done, and as a result, the

men had had no fresh meat, except ponies, since that time. In
short, it became clear when full news of the expedition leaked out,
that the Powder River fight was an example of an opportunity
thrown away in which every one was to blame, but not the rank
and file. Praise is due Captain Eagen, who carried out his orders
and charged through the village three times and it was ours as
we thought, but where was the support? Captain Noyes actually
allowed his men to unsaddle and rest after he had first driven
away the Indians' herd, and while the fighting was going on, and
for this he was afterwards court-martialed and reprimanded in
general orders. But the real trouble seems to have been simple
enough—a want of heart, excessive caution, especially the leader.
It was common to hear several of the men saying that if Custer
had had charge of this outfit he surely would have had the village,
and Indians and all, dead or alive, in half the time we were about
it, and then had to run away. Custer would probably have ended
in the complete distruction of the band of Crazy Horse, instead
of merely burning some of his property and exasperating him,
while all his horses were gone. It was an ominous commencement
for a campaign of disaster. After that time the curtain was hardly
ever lifted until the commencement of the winter's first start and
not in the form of a victory over hostile Indians, but the more
questionable success of a movement of far less danger that should
have been made long ago. This movement was the surrounding
and forcible disarmament of the Sioux at the principal agencies,
taking from them their ponies, and compelling them to live peaceably; and the army is fain to be proud of this, lacking other subjects of congratulation.

Recognizing fully the difficulties which surround army operations against the Indians, we must still admit the worst to be the
low character of the regular troops. In the infantry this is marked
by apparent inability to execute severe marches on foot; in the
cavalry by an almost total incapacity to fight mounted against the
Indians. Infantry and cavalry advance well enough in the common skirmish line on foot, but there are so many recruits, so few
veterans in the ranks, that the issue of single combat between Indian and dragoon is almost as a matter of course, the death of the
dragoon. From what I have seen there is a single remedy. It is
to teach the men how to use their sabres until they trust to them.
When officers and men do that the Indians will fear them and
not they the Indians.

After we received the order to retreat the Indians noticed what
we were doing and made a most furious attack, which added to
our wounded, myself getting a bowie-knife wound in the neck.

Now the Indians saw the two battalions advancing while they thought we had only one company, and then they retired quickly to the mountainsides again.

The village of Crazy Horse, at the Powder River, had 107 lodges, according to Major Stanton. He thought there would be between 300 and 400 men in that village. Now the proper military tactics would have been to surround that village, as the Indians did not seem to be on the alert as they ought to have been, not knowing where an enemy would spring from. The Indians did not even have a lookout on the high elevations and did not know of our presence until the charge through the village, and therefore would have made it one of the easiest military tactics to surround that village.

They could not escape up the rocks because the troops that were ordered up there to go along the ridge would have been able to fire on them if they offered any resistance, and their outlet would have been blocked by the troops in the valley.

A flag of truce, which I think might have been done by letting Major Stanton go in with a few of the scouts and come to some terms with Crazy Horse. Of course, all would have to be captured and arms taken away and marched to the nearest agency; but even that would have diminished Sitting Bull's force to a great extent and I believe would have been a great success and the country at large would have been more proud of the forces under Reynolds than a retreat as we had made instead of a victory.

Now Noyes and Mills were ordered to leave Reynolds' column and some of us who were badly wounded, and went to old Fort Phil Kearny to wait for the Crook column.

On the 7th of June, Crook's column was on the head of the Tongue River, near old Fort Phil Kearny, where, on the 8th, a war party of Sioux came down and tried to stampede the American horses, bringing on a skirmish which resulted in the repulse of the Indians. On the 14th the column was joined by a number of Crows and scouts, which they brought back and on the 16th, the whole party started to find the bands of Sitting Bull and Crazy Horse, reported to be on the Rosebud River, to the north. The Crows who came in reported that they had seen Gibbon's camp on the other side of the Sioux, on the Tongue River, and that the United States forces had already been attacked by Sitting Bull's people, who had taken some horses from them. Thus it will be seen that up to the 16th of June, the United States program was carried out as fairly as could be expected, and that two of the converging columns had already arrived within striking distance of Sitting Bull and his friends.

It was now that its faults were to be glaringly exposed. The regular force near the enemy amounted to 1,700 men, whereof 400 were separated from the other 1,300 by rough and mountainous country of some hundred miles, and between the two lay Sitting Bull and his braves, in a compact body. On the 16th, Crook advanced his force early in the morning. Each man carried four days' rations, the infantry were mounted on mules and train was left behind them. The destination of the column was Sitting Bull's village on the Rosebud River, sixty miles north. By the evening of the 16th, the column had marched forty miles and went into camp for the night. Now it looked to me like we should have marched some of the night and attacked at daybreak, but just as in the case of the Powder River fight, the time was lost. The mistake is claimed by the correspondent to be the fault of the Indian allies, who had been out hunting buffalo that day, and who gorged themselves with meat that night and refused to advance. A poor excuse is better than none. But there is a difference in this correspondent who tried to hide the fault of others. Sir Archibald Forbes, war correspondent of the London Times, would not favor private or general in such careless blunders.

The next morning Sitting Bull turned the tables and attacked Crook, and the story told by the correspondent is instructive. It shows what a tissue of blunders and cross-purposes a battle may become under the command of the oldest of generals in Indian warfare, when all are not animated by the same spirit. The Crows and other scouts had been sent forward to find the Sioux village, and the correspondent proceeds: "June 17, having marched seven miles, being in camp unsaddled, successive shots were heard, and the Sioux confirmed by our scouts pouring over the hills. Our present position, being surrounded by bluffs, was an untenable one, and one well chosen by the Sioux for their attack. The advance was sounded, and the line of battle then formed was Noyes' battalion, right; Mills', right center; Chambers', center; Indian allies, left center; Royall (with Henry's battalion and one company of Mills') left. Mills' and Noyes' battalions were pushed forward, charging the enemy in gallant style. The rest of the line did not advance. Mills and Noyes were ordered to march on the village, which order fortunately for them was revoked. Royall's right was separated from the main command by about a quarter of a mile. He occupied a very important and dangerous position; one which if held by the enemy would have rendered Crook's line on the bluff untenable, unless he had advanced. Having occupied this place under a heavy fire from the commencement of the fight (8:00 A. M.), Captain Nickerson of General Crook's staff brought (attended with great personal danger, as the Indians seemed to divine his mission) orders for Colonel Royall to retire or connect his line with General Crook's. This was effected, instead of by a forward movement, by a sort of left about wheel, or retreat. The Indians seized this favorable opportunity by advancing and occupying the place vacated by ourselves and pouring upon us a galling fire from three different directions, charging upon our lines and trying to capture our led horses, our men being dismounted as skirmishers. Royall, by maintaining successive lines of retreat, aided by the great gallantry of his men and officers, succeeded, with loss, in joining Crook's command. This loss was diminished by the charge made by our allies and two infantry companies from Crook's left upon the advancing Sioux. This charge should have been made when we first commenced our retreat movement. It was in what may be called "Death Hollow," during the retreat while superintending the movements of his battalion, that Colonel Henry was severely wounded in the face, the ball entering near the left temple and coming out the right side, and myself shot in the left arm. They had us in a bad fix.

The order now was for all the troops to advance upon the village, supposed to be some six miles off. This order was twice given and twice changed, the latter owing to ammunition becoming short, and upon the representation of the guide, who had lived with the Sioux for seven years, that it would be impossible to pass through a difficult canyon and secure the village without immense loss to our troops. These reasons, besides caring for his wounded, decided General Crook to go into camp on the battle field of the day, which he did. The next two succeeding days, without further molestation, we returned to our permanent camp.

Now I felt bad from the way things had gone. It was another Powder River disaster, and this the fault of those in command. Just think: An old Indian fighter being in camp unsaddled at the commencement of the fight, while on a march to "surprise" an active foe. In the course of the battle our flank was driven in with serious loss and only saved from annihilation by the charge of the Indian allies and the infantry, but even that cannot hide the fact of real defeat, I am sorry to say, for had we been successful, I would have asked permission to join Custer's column. The object of the scout, so unsuccessful and yet not without an encouraging result, was to discover and destroy the village of the Sioux, which the silent man advised Crook not to try to enter Sitting Bull's village, for it would mean immense loss to our troops. The Indians agreed in declaring to be on the Yellowstone River, between the mouths of the Rosebud and the Tongue river. It proved to be nearer the base of the expedition than was believed, and General Crook's ignorance of its proximity, due to the negligence and inactivity of the Crow allies, who were entrusted with the work of scouting, is the cause of failure of the movement. The Sioux were certainly repulsed in their bold onset and lost many of their bravest warriors, but when they fled could not be pursued without great danger in the rough country through which their way led. Had his scouts proved faithful, so that he could have been prepared to occupy the commanding position with infantry in advance of the main column he would have had warning of the concentration of the enemy to impede his course, and could have driven them back into the village and ended the campaign by destroying it. It will be seen that the blame of the miscarriage of the scout whose instinct, vigilance and knowledge of their own country was relied upon. The last sentence, "had it not been," etc., is decidedly good. It shows that Crook was outgeneraled by Sitting Bull, and that the latter had troops not accustomed to the direct charge and that is all.

The Indians fought in their own way, and did all they wanted. They drove Crook back to his camp.

CHAPTER V

It will be seen that the correspondent puts the very best face on the battle that could be put there, but none the less it is impossible to hide the fact that Crook was taken by surprise. "Being in camp unsaddled" is the commencement of the fight, while on a march to "surprise" an active foe. In the course of the battle, Crook's left is driven in with serious loss, and only saved from annihilation by the charges of the Indian allies and the infantry. The Herald correspondent puts on a still better face by claiming a substantial victory, but even he cannot hide the fact of real defeat. He says:

"The object of the scout was so unsuccessful and yet not without an encouraging result, was to discover and destroy the village of the Sioux, which the guides, white, half-breed and Indian, agreed in declaring to be on the Yellowstone River, between the mouths of the Rosebud and the Tongue. It proved to be nearer the base of the expedition than was believed, and General Crook's ignorance of its proximity, due to the negligence and inactivity of the Crow allies, who were entrusted with the work of scouting, is the cause of the failure of the movement.

The Sioux were certainly repulsed in their bold onset, and lost many of their bravest warriors, but when they fled could not be pursued without grave danger in the rough country through which their way lay. Had his scouts proved faithful, so that he could have been prepared to occupy the commanding positions with infantry in advance of the main column, he would have had warning of the concentration of the enemy to impede his course, and could have driven him back into the village and ended the campaign by destroying it. It will be seen that the blame of the miscarriage of the scout belongs to the Crows, whose instinct, vigilance and knowledge of their own country was relied upon to render every move of the force intelligent. On the contrary, their undisciplined frenzy and failure to discover the lodgement of the enemy in time to frustrate their meditated attack precipitated a battle which began with a stupendous advantage on his side and in a spot of his own choice, naturally suitable to the success of their method of warfare. The Sioux's strength was masked, except when, emboldened by the disastrous withdrawal of the left wing of the cavalry, they made a dash from both ends of a deep hollow which lay in its way and exposed it to a murderous fire, and suddenly swarmed on the front, left and rear. Then it was that the timely fire of the infantry upon their main body, the charge of the Snakes into the hollow and a rapid pursuit of them for three miles, dismayed them utterly and they fell back and disappeared. Had it not been for their occupation, unperceived by the General, of positions from which they could pour an enfilading fire upon both flanks of the body of cavalry on the left, they could not have stood in the face of the troops a moment after their first charge."

The last sentence, "had it not been," etc., is decidedly good. It shows that Crook was outgeneraled by Sitting Bull, and that the latter had troops not accustomed to the direct charge, and that is all. The Indians fought in their own way and did all they wanted. They drove Crook back to his camp.

Meanwhile, what were Terry and Gibbon doing? The reports show the following state of things:

Generals Terry and Gibbon communicated with each other, June 1st, near the junction of the Tongue and Yellowstone Rivers, and learned that a heavy force of Indians had concentrated on the opposite bank of the Yellowstone, but about eighteen miles distant. For fourteen days the Indian pickets had confronted Gibbon's videttes.

General Gibbon reported to General Terry that the cavalry had thoroughly scouted the Yellowstone as far as the mouth of the Big Horn and no Indians had crossed it. It was now certain that they were not prepared for them, and on the Powder, Tongue, Rosebud, Little Horn or Big Horn Rivers General Terry at once commenced feeling for them.

Major Reno, of the Seventh Cavalry, with six companies of that regiment, was sent up Powder River 150 miles to the mouth of Little Powder to look for the Indians, and, if possible, to communicate with General Crook. He reached the mouth of the Little Powder in five days, but saw no Indians and could hear nothing of Crook. As he returned, he found on the Rosebud a very large Indian trail, about nine days old, and followed it a short distance, when he turned about up Tongue River and reported to General Terry what he had seen. It was now known no Indians were on Tongue River or Powder River, and the net had narrowed down to Rosebud, Little Horn and Big Horn Rivers.

General Terry, who had been waiting with Custer and the steamer Far West at the mouth of Tongue River, for Reno's report, as soon as he heard it, ordered Custer to march up the south bank to a point opposite General Gibbon, who was encamped on the north bank of the Yellowstone. Terry, on board the steamer Far West, pushed up the Yellowstone, keeping abreast of General Custer's column.

General Gibbon was found in camp, quietly awaiting developments. A consultation was had with Generals Gibbon and Custer, and then General Terry definitely fixed upon the plan of action. It was believed the Indians were on the head of the Rosebud or over on the Little Horn, a divide or ridge only fifteen miles wide separating the two streams. It was announced by General Terry that General Custer's column would strike the blow.

In order to understand the position of affairs, it will now be necessary to lay before the reader an outline sketch of the lines of the campaign so far, and show the position of the contending parties at this time. (See map.) This sketch indicates with sufficient accuracy for the reader the progress of the campaign. It shows the routes of the three columns up to the juncture when Custer was sent after the Indians, and the lines of march. It will be seen that after Gibbon's and Terry's junction the two were about a hundred miles from Crook, and that the Sioux were between them. Crook, after his defeat, fell back to the head of the Tongue River. The Powder, Tongue, Rosebud and Big Horn Rivers all run north into the Yellowstone, and Sitting Bull was between the headwaters of the Rosebud and Big Horn, the main tributary of the latter being known as the Little Big Horn. Thus stood matters when Terry sent off the following dispatch to Sheridan from his camp at the mouth of the Rosebud River. He writes:

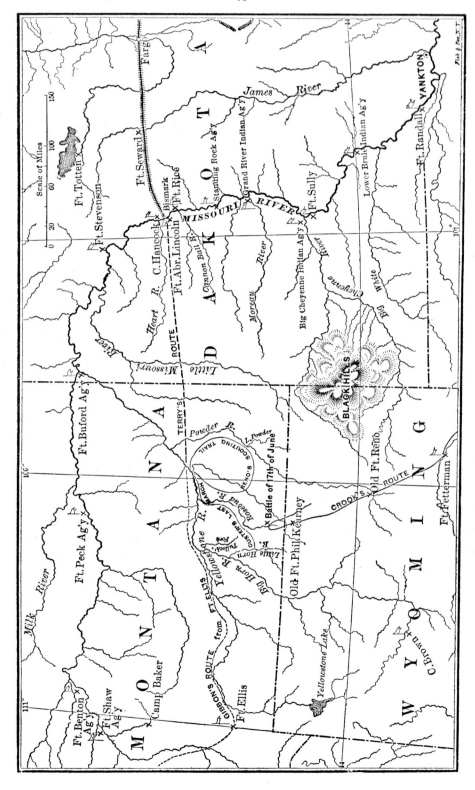

"No Indians have been met with as yet, but traces of two large and recent camps have been discovered twenty or thirty miles up the Rosebud. Gibbon's column will move this morning on the north side of the Yellowstone, for the mouth of the Big Horn, where it will be ferried across by the supply steamer, and whence it will proceed to the mouth of the Little Horn, and so on. Custer will go up the Rosebud tomorrow with his whole regiment, and thence to the headwaters of the Little Horn, thence down the Little Horn."

CHAPTER VI

The Last Battle

Before entering on the consideration of Custer's last march and battle, it is necessary to correct a mistaken impression set afloat by those same insincere friends and real enemies who had already done their best to embroil and embitter the close of his life. This impression is that Custer, during the whole of the last campaign, was suffering from depression of spirits, that he felt his disgrace keenly, that he was slighted by General Terry, and that these stings induced him to act rashly. The facts are exactly the reverse.

General Terry, from the very commencement of the expedition, trusted Custer implicitly, and the very best feeling existed between them. No one was more modest than Terry, nor more willing to defer to the experience of Custer; and inasmuch as the route followed by the Terry column was the very same as that followed three years before by the Stanley expedition, General Terry was only too glad to avail himself of Custer's help to pilot the column, just as Stanley had in his time. It became Custer's regular duty to ride ahead of the main body with a battalion of the Seventh Cavalry and to mark out the day's march for the wagons by leaving a broad trail. An officer, present during the whole campaign, whose name we at present withhold, says:

"As he seemed to me first, so he was to the last—the incarnation of energy. How often I watched him in our march to the Powder River, like the thoroughbred he rode, champing the bit and chafing to be off, longing for action. Our last day's march before reaching Powder River was through the worst and roughest country that I have ever seen a train taken over in campaign.

"Early in the day the guides and scouts were baffled by the labyrinth of ravines and confusion of bad lands. Custer took the lead and took us through. I heard General Terry express his satisfaction that evening in these words: 'No one but General Custer could have brought us through. He is the best guide I ever saw.' Notwithstanding his manifestation of a little restiveness during this march, I was glad to know that he was steadily revealing his fine qualities to General Terry, and winning his way to the position which drew from his commanding officer the carte blanche under which he marched up the Rosebud on the 22d of June. It will not do for anyone to say that he disobeyed orders on that occasion. He did as every one capable of comprehending him and his orders knew that he would do, and by those orders I am willing that he shall be judged, not by documents or explanations outside of them."

The reader will now very naturally ask to see these orders and find what they were. Fortunately, they exist, and are as follows:

"LIEUT. COL. CUSTER, Seventh Cavalry:

"Colonel:—The Brigadier General commanding directs that as soon as your regiment can be made ready for the march you proceed up the Rosebud in pursuit of the Indians whose trail was discovered by Major Reno a few days since. It is, of course, impossible to give any definite instructions in regard to this movement, and, were it not impossible to do so, the Department Commander places too much confidence in your zeal, energy and ability to wish to impose upon you precise orders which might hamper your action when nearly in contact with the enemy. He will, however, indicate to you his own views of what your action should be, and he desires that you should conform to them unless you shall see sufficient reason for departing from them. He thinks that you should proceed up the Rosebud until you ascertain definitely the direction in which the trail above spoken of leads. Should it be found, as it appears to be almost certain that it will be found, to turn toward the Little Big Horn, he thinks that you should still proceed southward, perhaps, as far as the headwaters of the Tongue, and then turn toward the Little Big Horn, feeling constantly, however, to your left so as to preclude the possibility of the escape of the Indians to the south or southeast by passing around your left flank. The column of Col. Gibbon is now in motion for the mouth of the Big Horn. As soon as it reaches that point it will cross the Yellowstone and move up at least as far as the parks of the Big and Little Big Horn. Of course, its future movements must be controlled by circumstances as they arise; but it is hoped that the Indians, if upon the Little Big Horn, may be so nearly inclosed by two columns that their escape will be impossible. The Department Commander desires that on your way up the Rosebud you should thoroughly examine the upper part of Tulloch's Creek, and that you should endeavor to send a scout through to Col. Gibbon's column with information of the result of your examination. The lower part of this creek will be examined by a detachment from Col. Gibbon's command. The supply steamer will be pushed up the Big Horn as far as the forks of the river are found navigable for that space, and the Department Commander, who will accompany the column of Col. Gibbon, desires you to report to him there not later than the expiration of the time for which your troops are rationed, unless in the meantime you receive further orders.

"Respectfully, etc.,

"E. W. SMITH, Captain 18th Infantry,
"Acting Assistant Adjutant General."

These orders are quite clear and explicit on one subject. Custer was sent out to find the Indians by following their trail up the Rosebud, and Gibbon was to hunt them from another direction, first, up the Yellowstone, then up the Big Horn River. This would bring the two columns together on the Big Horn somewhere to the south of the place where the battle finally occurred, if both moved at the same rate, for their trails would then be each round two sides of a rectangle, from corner to corner. The first corner was the junction of the Rosebud and Yellowstone; the opposite one, Sitting Bull's village on the Big Horn. Nothing, however, was said in the order about rates of marching, and Custer was left entirely to his own discretion as to what he should do if he struck the enemy first. The only limit placed to his time in the order is the period for which his troops are rationed. That period was fifteen days. The only expression of opinion on future movements is found in the sentence, "It is hoped that the Indians, if upon the Little Big Horn, may be so nearly enclosed by the two columns that escape may be impossible." The only fear of Terry seems to be that the Indians will escape. On Custer's way up the Rosebud, he is directed to examine "the upper part of Tulloch's Creek." This creek runs into the Big Horn near its mouth. Its "upper part" was some ten miles to the right of Custer's actual trail, which followed that of the Indian village previously found by Reno. Custer was to "endeavor to send through a scout to Colonel Gibbon's column." If he found that the trail turned (as it did) to the right, Terry "thinks you should still proceed southward" to the headwaters of the Tongue before turning after the Indians. All these instructions, it will be noticed, are entirely advisory and permissory, not peremptory. Terry expresses his conviction of the impossibility of giving any precise orders "which might hamper your action when nearly in contact with the enemy," and only desires Custer to conform to his views "unless you shall see sufficient reason for departing from them." It is quite clear on the face of these orders that Custer cannot be held legally or morally responsible for any departure from Terry's advice. The whole matter is left entirely in his discretion, the general placing "too much confidence in your zeal, energy and ability" to give any orders, beyond one to report in fifteen days. Upon his discretion solely he must be judged. In following him through the course of this his last march, we shall embody so much of the official report of his second in command, Major Reno, made at the close of the operations, as covers the period of Custer's death, illustrating it by the evidence of other persons, taken since that time. This report is valuable on account of its presumed reliability as to dates, times and places. It was first published in the Army and Navy Journal of New York City, the official Army paper, and is addressed, according to military etiquette, to the chief of Terry's staff for the time being. It commences as follows:

"Headquarters, Seventh Cavalry,
"Camp on Yellowstone River, July 5, 1876.

"CAPTAIN E. W. SMITH, A. D. C. and A. A. A. G.:

"The command of the regiment having devolved upon me, as the senior surviving officer from the battle of June 25th and 26th, between the Seventh Cavalry and Sitting Bull's band of hostile Sioux, on the Little Big Horn River, I have the honor to submit the following report of its operations from the time of leaving the main column until the command was united in the vicinity of the Indian village.

"The regiment left the camp at the mouth of the Rosebud River, after passing in review before the Department Commander, under command of Brevet Major General G. A. Custer, lieutenant colonel, on the afternoon of the 22d of June, and marched up the Rosebud twelve miles and encamped. 23d. Marched up the Rosebud, passing many old Indian camps and following a very large lodge-pole trail, but not fresh, making thirty-three miles, and we then encamped and waited for information from the scouts. At 9:25 P. M. Custer called the officers together and informed us that, beyond a doubt, the village was in the valley of the Little Big Horn, and that to reach it, it was necessary to cross the divide between Rosebud and Little Big Horn, and it would be impossible to do so in the daytime, without discovering our march to the Indians; that we would prepare to move at 11 P. M. This was done, the line of march turning from the Rosebud to the right, up one of its branches, which headed near the summit of the divide.

"About 2 A. M. of the 25th the scouts told him that he could not cross the divide before daylight. We then made coffee and rested for three hours, at the expiration of which time the march was resumed, the divide crossed, and about 8 A. M. the command was in the valley of one of the branches of the Little Big Horn. By this time Indians had been seen, and it was certain that we could not surprise them, and it was determined to move at once to the attack.

"Previous to this no division of the regiment had been made since the order was issued, on the Yellowstone, annulling wing and battalion organizations. General Custer informed me he would assign commands on the march. I was ordered by Lieutenant W. W. Cook, adjutant, to assume command of Companies M, A and G; Captain Benteen of Companies H, D and K; Custer retaining C, E, F, I and L under his immediate command, and Company B, Captain McDougall, in rear of the pack train. I assumed command of the companies assigned me, and without any definite orders moved forward with the rest of the column, and well to its left. I saw Benteen moving further to the left, and, as they passed, he told me he had orders to move well to the left and sweep everything before him; I did not see him again until about 2:30 P. M. The command moved down the creek towards the Little Big Horn Valley. Custer, with five companies on the right bank; myself and three companies on the left bank, and Benteen farther to the left, and out of sight."

Here we must pause awhile. Major Reno, Brevet Colonel Benteen and President Grant have made the pause necessary by official accusations of Custer's action up to this point. Major Reno, near the close of his report, accuses Custer in these words:

"I think (after the great number of Indians there were in the village) that the following reasons obtained for the misfortune: His rapid marching for two days and one night before the fight, attacking in the daytime at 12 M., and when they were on the qui vive, instead of early in the morning, and, lastly, his unfortunate division of the regiment into three commands."

General Terry, in a subsequent dispatch to Sheridan, quoting

Benteen, accuses Custer of the same fault, and states that Custer had told him that his marches "would be at the rate of thirty miles a day."

Custer, according to Reno's report, left Terry at noon, 22d June, and struck Sitting Bull on the morning of June 25th, having made one night march only. On the face of Reno's report, the night march was only from 11 P. M. to 2 A. M., or three hours. Then came a rest of three hours, with feed for man and horse, the march resumed at 5 A. M., the Indians seen at 8 A. M., finally struck at 12:30. This gives a period of three whole days in all, at 30 miles a day, making 90 miles. The actual distance, measured on the best accessible map, makes the length of Custer's trail just 90 miles; and we can afford to allow 10 more for windings. According to Reno's report, the distance marched to the evening of the 24th June was 73 miles (12+33+28), leaving only 27 miles for the distance covered during the following night and day march. In Terry's dispatch of self-justification, above referred to, he says, "I learned from Captain Benteen that on the 22d the cavalry marched 12 miles; on the 23d, 25 miles; from 5 A. M. till 8 P. M. of the 24th, 45 miles, and then after night 10 miles further, resting but without unsaddling, 23 miles to the battlefield." This account adds just 15 miles to the actual distance. It also subtracts eight miles from Reno's report of the march of the 23d June, and puts on 17 miles to Reno's account of the march of the 24th. Where Reno says 33, Terry, quoting Benteen, says 25; where Reno says 28, Terry, quoting Benteen, says 45.

President Grant, who hated Custer, as he had reason to, having injured him, distorts the facts still more in his published interview with a Herald correspondent, months after. We give this part of the interview entire, question and answer:

Correspondent—Was not Custer's massacre a disgraceful defeat of our troops?

The President (with an expression of manifest and keenly felt regret)—I regard Custer's massacre as a sacrifice of troops, brought on by Custer himself, that was wholly unnecessary—wholly unnecessary.

Correspondent—How so, Mr. President?

The President—He was not to have made the attack before effecting a junction with Terry and Gibbon. He was notified to meet them on the 26th, but instead of marching slowly, as his orders required, in order to effect the junction on the 26th, he enters upon a forced march of eighty-three miles in twenty-four hours, and thus had to meet the Indians alone on the 25th.

Thus Reno, who, whatever his faults, is apparently an honorable man, who labors to tell the truth, makes the whole march of the 24th and 25th June only 55 miles (28+27), agreeing with the map; Terry, quoting Benteen, makes it 78 miles (45+10+-23); Grant, the President, in his eagerness to bury a dead man out of sight, makes it 83 miles.

On the face of Reno's report, and compared with the actual distance, judging Custer as we have a right to, solely on his "zeal, energy and ability," not on supposed orders, which Terry's written instructions prove he never received, it appears that so far he had done everything that a cool and wary Indian fighter could have done. At all events, the Indians had not escaped. Let us see now what followed, still quoting Reno. His report proceeds thus:

"As we approached a deserted village, in which was standing one tepee, about 11 A. M., Custer motioned me to cross to him, which I did, and moved nearer to his column, until about 12:30 A. M., when Lieutenant Cook, adjutant, came to me and said the village was only two miles ahead and running away. To 'move forward at as rapid gait as I thought prudent and to charge afterwards, and the whole outfit would support me.' I think those were his exact words. I at once took a fast trot and moved down about two miles, when I came to a ford of the river. I crossed immediately and halted about ten minutes or less to gather the battalion, sending word to Custer that I had everything in front of me and that they were strong.

"I deployed, and with the Ree scouts on my left, charged down the valley, driving the Indians with great ease for about 2½ miles. I, however, soon saw that I was being drawn into some trap, as they certainly would fight harder, and especially as we were nearing their village, which was still standing; besides, I could not see Custer* or any other support, and at the same time the very earth seemed to grow Indians, and they were running towards me in swarms and from all directions. I saw I must defend myself and give up the attack mounted. This I did, taking possession of a point of woods, and which furnished, near its edge, a shelter for the horses; dismounted, and fought them on foot, making headway through the wood. I soon found myself in the near vicinity of the village, saw that I was fighting odds of

---

* This fact, of not seeing Custer, evidently frightened Reno excessively, and his story shows how unfit he was to take part in any operation requiring combined efforts. Had he gone on, as he was ordered, he would have found Custer supporting him, in the most effective manner possible, by attacking the enemy in rear.

at least five to one, and that my only hope was to get out of the wood, where I would soon have been surrounded, and gain some high ground. I accomplished this by mounting and charging the Indians between me and the bluffs, on the opposite side of the river. In this charge, First Lieutenant Donald McIntosh, Second Lieutenant Ben H. Hodgson, Seventh Cavalry, and A. A. Surg. J. M. De Wolf were killed. I succeeded in reaching the top of the bluff, with a loss of three officers and twenty-nine enlisted men killed, and seven men wounded. Almost at the same time I reached the top, mounted men were seen to be coming towards us, and it proved to be Colonel Benteen's battalion, Companies H, D and K; we joined forces and in a short time the pack train came up. As senior, my command was then Companies A, B, D, G, H, K and M, about 380 men, and the following officers: Captains Benteen, Weir, French and McDougall, First Lieutenants Godfrey, Mathey and Gibson, Second Lieutenants Edgerly, Wallace, Varnum and Hare; A. A. Surg. Porter. First Lieutenant De Rudio was in the dismounted fight in the woods, but having some trouble with his horse, did not join the command in the charge out, and, hiding himself in the woods, joined the command after nightfall of the 26th.

"Still hearing nothing of Custer, and with this reinforcement, I moved down the river in the direction of the village, keeping on the bluffs. We had heard firing in that direction, and knew it could only be Custer. I moved to the summit of the highest bluff, but seeing and hearing nothing, sent Captain Weir with his company to open communication with the other command. He soon sent back word, by Lieutenant Hare, that he could go no farther, and that the Indians were getting around him; at this time he was keeping up a heavy fire from his skirmish line. I at once turned everything back to the first position I had taken on the bluff, and which seemed to me the best. I dismouetnd the men, had the horses and mules of the pack train driven together in a depression, put the men on the crests of the hills making the depression, and had hardly done so when I was furiously attacked; this was about 6 P. M.; we held our ground with the loss of eighteen enlisted men killed and forty-six wounded, until the attack ceased, about 9 P. M."

A perusal of the first part of this account will show that whatever the length of the previous marches, the horses in Reno's column were not so fagged out but what they could make "a fast trot" for two miles to the ford, and then drive the Indians two and a half miles further. This makes nearly five miles at a fast pace in column or in ranks; with packed saddles and exhausted horses they could not have done that.

The next point to be considered is that of dividing the regiment into three commands. Here Custer is again blamed by Reno at the close of his report, as well as in a letter which the author lately received from him, totally unsolicited, and in which he tries to justify his conduct. In the report he calls it "his unfortunate division of the regiment into three commands;" in the letter he says "The division of the regiment into three separate and independent commands he was responsible for, and must always be held so."

It will be here observed by those who have read this history through that Custer's invariable method of attack on an enemy was the same which he adopted on the Big Horn, an attack on front and flank at all events, both flanks and front if possible, from all sides at once if he had time to execute it. In every battle in the Civil War, when he was in an independent position, he always worked his command by fractions, so as to attack the enemy on several points at once, and always succeeded, because he was always heartily seconded by men who adored him. He counted much on the moral effect to be produced on an enemy by combined attacks and a cross-fire, and always found his calculations correct. In fact, only one thing could vitiate them. This was cowardice or disobedience in the leader of any of the fractions which were to work simultaneously; and this misfortune Custer had never hitherto suffered. His subordinates were used to being put into tight places, where everything at first seemed hopeless, trusting implicitly to their leader's combinations to get them out.

Next, were these commands independent? We can hardly see that, any more than regimental commanders are independent in a brigade. No general can do anything if his colonels will not support him; no colonel can fight a cavalry regiment under Upton's tactics if his battalion commanders slight, disobey or even misunderstand his orders. Custer was a peculiar man. He fought in a peculiar way, and needed to have men under him used to his rapid, energetic style, and who understood him. Did Reno understand him, and was he used to him? The official record says not. He had never served under Custer in the field, nor seen an Indian fight since the Civil War.

Let us see whether he supported Custer. He says he "charged down the valley, driving the Indians with great ease for about two and one-half miles." Then he suddenly stops. Why? He says he "saw he was being drawn into some trap." An officer, present with the expedition, who examined the ground, but whose name we prefer to withhold for the present, writes as follows:

4

"He (Reno) marched until he came to the village, dismounted, and occupied a timber bottom, which completely sheltered him and his horses. Girard (the interpreter) says, corroborated by Herndon (a scout), 'Not many Indians in sight at this time, and firing at 500 and 600 yards.' So long was the range that Charley Reynolds, another scout, said, 'No use firing at this range; we will have a better chance by and by.' An officer present says that Reno mounted and dismounted, and then mounted again in hot haste, and made what figures in his report as a "charge." He is the only person I have heard call it by that name. The surgeon present says there was only one man wounded before Reno abandoned the timber, and his loss begun when he was making the charge, men and horses shot from behind. Think of the charge they must have made, across the Little Horn, and were checked in their flight by Benteen running into them. I say running into them, because it was mere accident. But where was Custer? He moved down to the lower end of the village from three to four miles. How long did Reno engage the Sioux village? Not over thirty minutes. What is the conclusion? That Reno was in and out of the fight before Custer was engaged. If further proof is wanting, it is found in the fact that Reno says in his report he heard Custer's firing from the top of the hill to which he had retreated.

Besides the letter from which this extract is taken, the author has received a letter from another officer present with Major Reno, in response to one asking several detailed and specific questions as to the fight in the bottom, the subsequent halt on the hill, and the possibility of cooperation with Custer on the part of Reno and Benteen. This letter is especially valuable, because written with Major Reno's sanction and knowledge, and representing his side of the question as fully as could be desired. In the expression of opinion on probabilities, this officer coincides with Reno, but his facts corroborate those stated by the other officer, whose opinions are exactly opposite. The facts furnished by Major Reno's friend are as follows:

"At the time Reno ceased his forward movement, no man had been killed or wounded, but the cloud of dust denoted an immense number of Indians a short way off, and several times that number between us and that cloud, which was over the village, advancing in their peculiar manner and passing to our left and rear. * * * The command was dismounted, the horses placed in a wood, and the men deployed on foot across the plain. The number of Indians continued to increase and to surround us. Colonel Reno ordered us to prepare to mount, which, of course, took every one to the wood. We were mounted as though to charge, and in an instant afterward dismounted, and I supposed we were to fight it out here, when a fire opened from the rear through the brush. * * * We were ordered to mount. I was by the side of Colonel Reno, going out of the wood, and asked if we were to charge through. He said yes, and the command moved, Colonel Reno leading. I was here separated from the command for a time, and on turning towards it, saw it moving towards the ford that led to the hill. The column was fighting at close range from all sides. I rejoined with difficulty, and followed close along the rear to the ford, and here the confusion began. Previously, the men had kept in column, using their pistols. When the ford was reached, it was each man for himself. In passing up the hill, beyond the river, horses and men were joined together, and some of the hindmost suffered necessarily."

So far, as to the facts of the fight in the bottom, Reno's friend even exceeds the testimony of Reno's harshest critics as to his incapacity and utter demoralization during the attack of the Indians. We have italicized the places of most importance, as they tell the real story. "Advancing in their peculiar manner"— what does this mean in plain English? That the Indians were all at full speed, crouching over the necks of their fleet little ponies, flogging away with their short whips, and all the time yelling out their "Hi—yip—yip—yip—hi yah," firing random bullets in the air. These sights and sounds seem to have deprived Reno of all presence of mind. This he shows clearly by his repeated changes of policy, mounting and dismounting four times in as many minutes and finally charging out in column, firing pistols, said column speedily becoming a huddled mass of frightened fugitives.

As to the halt on the hill, this officer differs materially with Reno and Benteen in point of time. He admits hearing a few shots down the stream, but no heavy firing, and states that it was an hour before Benteen arrived, and half an hour more before the packs came up, whereas Benteen and Reno both agree that they came together almost immediately after Reno's action. In this manner it is pretty clear that the recollection of Major Reno's friend must deceive him, as he places Weir's advance almost immediately after the junction, and it is clear from Reno's report that Weir must have started out after 5 o'clock, for it was only fifteen minutes from his return to the beginning of the siege on the hill (at 6 P. M.), on Reno's showing. This officer, like Benteen, thinks that Custer had been destroyed by the time Benteen arrived on the hill, whereas Kill Eagle's evidence, subsequently mentioned, shows that this was not the case till sunset.

He makes one curious assertion in giving his estimate of the Indian warriors, which he places at 3,500. It is this: "In a village, standing, squaws, old men and boys, are as effective as the ordinary recruit." Endorsing such opinions, is it any wonder Reno's battalion was beaten, when they are ready to succumb to squaws, old men and boys?

Now let us return to Reno's report and try it by the test of time and place. He says that Adjutant Cook told him to attack at 12:30; that he advanced altogether four and one-half miles, crossed a river, halted ten minutes, had his fight, and came back, meeting Benteen. When did he meet Benteen? Look back to the report. He there says of Benteen, "I did not see him again till about 2:30 P. M." That gives two hours for his advance of four and one-half miles, fording the river twice, driving the enemy two and one-half miles and the dismounted fight. Our period of thirty minutes for the fight in the bottom seems to tally with Reno's report. It is clear that it was a short fight, and Reno confesses his overcaution in the words, "I saw that I was being drawn into some trap."

The next question is, how long did Reno remain on the hill with his seven companies, in safety and unassailed? Here again his report helps us. He met Benteen at 2:30 P. M.; he was "furiously attacked; this was about 6 P. M." The time is thus complete. Three hours and a half of waiting on the hill, listening to Custer's volleys, and not a step taken to renew the attack. Another piece of evidence is found in the narrative of Herndon, the scout, who was with Reno. When the major "charged" out, Herndon's horse fell and threw him, then ran away, leaving him in the bush, where he was joined by thirteen soldiers, three of them wounded and left behind. His story was published in all the papers, but I quote from the Army and Navy Journal of July 15, 1876, as a semi-official paper, and the one chosen by Reno for publication of his report. Statements in that paper on army subjects are apt to be more reliable than elsewhere, as, being the only professional paper in the country, all army officers watch its columns and correct every mistake. Herndon says of the "charge" which he saw from the timber, "Little resistance was offered, and it was a complete rout to the ford. I did not see the men at the ford and do not know what took place, further than a good many were killed when the command left the timber." Herndon and his thirteen comrades remained in the timber unmolested for nearly three hours after Reno's flight, hearing firing down the river about two miles, while nearly all the Indians in their front left and went down the valley. Then the little party got out and went to Reno, meeting only a roving group of five Indians, whom they beat off, then crossed the river to Reno. In fifteen minutes after, the siege on the hill commenced."*

What should Reno have done? His only real safety was to hug the timber and defend himself, surrounded or not. Custer had done so on the Yellowstone in 1873, ninety against three hundred; Robbins had done even better in defending his wagons in 1867, forty against six hundred. In both these cases there was no apparent hope of succor coming, and yet Robbins and Custer found the reward of their tenacity, help coming when it was least expected and victory following. On Reno's own statement, he had one hundred and forty-five men, who, in a circle, lining the edge of the wood, could have held it for hours. The Indians were fighting mounted, and could never have stormed the wood, and help was coming. Custer had promised to come. If Reno could get no further he could at least defend himself, die in his tracks if need be, like a soldier. Instead of this, he tried to escape by running away from an enemy who had the advantage in speed and who could ride alongside of the demoralized cavalry, pouring in perfect streams of bullets from their Winchester rifles. By his inexperience in Indian warfare, Major Reno thus gave himself up, helpless, to the favorite style of fighting of his enemies, whereas, in their superior horsemanship and superior arms, had a full chance to assert themselves. Looking for personal security, he took the course least adapted to secure it.

The Major, indeed, seems, from his hesitating movements in the fight, mounting and dismounting, to have been quite overwhelmed from the first by the novelty of his position, cowed by the fierce yells and rapid charge of the Indians, and finally to have completely lost his head. For all this we wish it distinctly understood that we do not deem Reno so blamable, as for subsequent event. It was his first Indian fight, and many a man has done badly in his first fight, who has afterwards succeeded. We should not have occasion to dissect his conduct in the affair were it not for that unjust sentence in his official report in which he throws the blame of a disaster, brought on by his own incapacity, on the shoulders of his dead chief. The facts shown by himself in the same report, illustrated by eye-witnesses, pass a different verdict on his actions.

But now, where was Benteen all the time of this fight? His

---

* Lieutenant de Rudio, mentioned in Reno's report, was also left behind and remained in the wood, together with Mr. Girard (the interpreter), Private O'Neil, and a half-breed scout. All these four got off, some that night, some next night. De Rudio's account shows a general careless, haphazard state of things among the Indians, entirely opposed to any deliberate trap or generalship.

own statement, published in the New York Herald, gives his movements. It seems that when he was sent out on the left bank of the stream with orders to sweep everything, he found no Indians, and that he recrossed the stream and rejoined the main trail. He says, "the whole time occupied in this march was about an hour and a half," to the main trail, about three miles from the point where Reno came back over the ford. From Major Reno's statement in the same paper, in reply to a letter of General Rosser, we learn that the division into battalions which sent Benteen off to the left was made at half-past ten A. M. An hour and a half brings us to noon and Benteen within three miles of the battlefield. At 12:30 Reno was ordered by Cook, the adjutant, to attack, and trotted off. At this time Benteen says:

"About three miles from the point where Reno crossed the ford I met a sergeant bringing orders to the commanding officer of the rear guard, Captain McDougall, Company B, to hurry up the pack trains. A mile further I was met by my trumpeter, bringing a written order from Lieutenant Cook, the adjutant of the regiment, to this effect: 'Benteen, come on; big village; be quick; bring packs.' And a postscript saying 'Bring packs.' A mile or a mile and a half further on, I first came in sight of the valley and Little Big Horn. About twelve or fifteen dismounted men were fighting on the plain with Indians, charging and recharging them. This body (the Indians) numbered about 900 at this time. Colonel Reno's mounted party were retiring across the river to the bluffs. I did not recognize till later what part of the command this was, but was clear that they had been beaten. I then marched my command in line to their succor. On reaching the bluff I reported to Colonel Reno, and first learned that the command had been separated, and that Custer was not in that part of the field, and no one of Reno's command was able to inform me of the whereabouts of General Custer."

Reno's report states that he met Benteen at 2:30 P. M. It seems thus that it took Benteen two hours and a half to cover a distance of three miles. What was he doing all this time? One incident, furnished us by an officer who was present, shows.

With Custer on this campaign was his brother, Boston Custer, who was the civilian forage master of the column. It seems that Boston Custer came to the rear during this period, went to the pack train, in rear of Benteen, got a fresh horse, and passed Benteen on his way back, speaking to some of the officers. Benteen was then watering his horses. Where did he water? He could only have done it at one place, where he crossed the river.

that is, three miles above the ford where he met Reno. Boston
Custer had time to get back to the General and be killed in the
fight. Benteen kept on at a slow pace. Did he obey the order,
"Benteen, come on; big village; be quick; bring packs"? What
did this order direct from Custer mean? What could it mean,
but that Custer wanted every man in his fight? He had sent in
Reno, and he needed Benteen's battalion and the company guard-
ing the packs with himself. That this was his intention is proved
by Reno, in his letter to Rosser, in these words:

"Trumpeter Martin, of Company H, and who the last time of
any living person heard and saw General Custer, and who brought
the last order his adjutant, Colonel Cook, ever penciled, says he
left the General at the summit of the highest bluff on that side,
and which overlooked the village and my first battlefield, and as he
turned, General Custer raised his hat and gave a yell, saying they
were asleep in their tepees and surprised, and to charge. Cook's
order (Custer's order, through his adjutant), sent to Benteen,
and which I afterwards saw and read, said, 'Big village; big
thing; bring up the packs.'"

Thus Benteen and Reno both unite in ascribing the same plan
to Custer, that of charging with all his force from two points.
Both admit by their testimony that they disobeyed orders. Reno
was ordered to "charge." He obeyed by opening a hesitating
skirmish and then running away. Benteen was ordered to "come
on; be quick." He obeyed by advancing three miles in two hours
and joining Reno in a three hours' halt. The order to "come on"
was from Custer, not Reno. Benteen made, on his own statement,
no effort to obey it. He might have known where Custer was.
Reno lets that much out. Benteen could have questioned Trumpeter Martin, who brought the order. No, he stopped, and let
his chief perish.

Looking at all the testimony impartially from this distance of
time, the conduct of Benteen is far worse than that of Reno. The
Major did his best in his fight, and it was nothing but want of
experience in command and in Indian warfare that caused his defeat. Benteen's case is different. He was an old Indian fighter,
a man of remarkable personal courage, as he proved in the subsequent battle, had fought under Custer, and knew his business perfectly. That he should have, as his own testimony confesses, deliberately disobeyed the peremptory order of Custer to "come on"
argues either a desire to sacrifice Custer or an ignorance of which
his past career renders him incapable.

There is a great difference between the words "big thing" and "be quick," and I am inclined to believe that the expression "big thing" is an after-thought of Major Reno's, as tending to confirm the notion which he inculcates all through his report and evidence, that Custer ran into a trap and was full of rash eagerness. Benteen got the order and he says it was "be quick," and that "bring packs" was repeated.

Custer told him to "come on," and he "reported to Colonel Reno." Well, then, it may be said, what did Benteen, afterwards? The rest of his testimony shows what he did. He says:

"While the command was awaiting the arrival of the pack mules, a company was sent forward in the direction supposed to have been taken by Custer. After proceeding about a mile, they were attacked and driven back. During this time I heard no heavy firing, and there was nothing to indicate that a heavy fight was going on, and I believe that at this time Custer's immediate command had been annihilated."

The rest of the story you must get from Colonel Reno, as he took command and knows more than any one else.

It is curious in Benteen's evidence how his only estimate of time comes in before the battle. Afterwards, there is not a word about time. Who would think that this brief paragraph covered from 2:30 to 6 P. M.? If the one company was sent forward, why was it not supported by the whole outfit? Why was Custer left alone with his battalion, while the other battalions were out of danger?

The answer to the question is given by Reno and Benteen in their evidence, almost unassisted by others. The reasons were, Reno's incapacity and Benteen's disobedience.

We have now examined Reno and Benteen. It is time to go to Custer. Where was Custer during all this time, from 12:30 to 6 P. M.? Let Reno, Terry and the trail answer, assisted by Trumpeter Martin, the last white man who saw Custer alive; Curly, the Upsaroka scout, the last living being of his column; and Kill Eagle, an Indian chief who was in Sitting Bull's camp, who has since come into Standing Rock Agency to surrender, and has given evidence.

Reno, in his letter, says that Custer, after leaving him, "moved rapidly down the river to the ford, at which he attempted to cross." Curly, the Crow scout, calls it about four miles, and such the trail shows it, on account of the winding of the ravines. Reno's advance was about two and one-half miles in a diagonal line. Consequently his skirmish line at the edge of the woods was not over two miles from the ford which Custer tried to cross. The

Indian village was three and one-half miles long, and Custer struck it about the middle. When did he strike it? We get this from the examination of Kill Eagle, published in the New York Herald of October 6th, 1876. The deposition was taken by Captain Johnston, First Infantry, acting Indian agent. We extract all that concerns the fight:

"The troops struck our trail on the tributary, followed it down, swam their horses over the Greasy Grass Creek and struck the camp at the upper end, where there was a clump of timber. On the southwest end of the camp they dismounted and tied their horses in the timber and opened the fight. When the firing commenced, the Indians rushed to the scene of action. I and my men were lower down, about the middle of the camp. The Indians drove the soldiers back out of the timber and they crossed the Greasy Grass Creek below the mouth of the tributary, taking their position on the high hills, bare without any grass. There they were reinforced by the soldiers who had not crossed the creek (Colonel Benteen and Captain McDougall). Before retreating across the creek the soldiers (Colonel Reno) got into the camp and set fire to some of the lodges. On retreating across the creek to take position on the hill, they left their dead behind them. Another party appeared on top of a long hill moving toward the south.

"After quitting the party on the knolls, word came that soldiers were on the left across the creek, and there was great excitement in the camp, the Indian warriors rushing to the left to meet the troops. The Indians crossed the creek and then the firing commenced. It was very fast at times, then slower until it died away. (He describes the firing as follows: He claps the palms of his hands together very fast for several minutes, stopping suddenly, which denotes the sound of the firing when they (Custer) first began. After a few seconds elapses he repeats the same as above and continues, but all the time lessens the quickness of the patting and sound until it gradually dies out.) The United States troops were all killed on the east side, none crossed the stream."

I got the following information from Sitting Bull himself: After crossing the creek with his warriors he met the troops (Custer) about 600 yards east of the river. He drove the soldiers back up the hill. He then made a circuit to the right around the hill and drove off and captured most of the horses. The troops made a stand at the lower end of the hill, and there they were all killed. In going around the hill the Cheyenne Indians killed a warrior, thinking he was a scout who left this agency; but he was not; he was a hostile.

Q. How long did the fight last on the right?

A. It was about noon when they (Reno) struck the camp, and it only lasted a few minutes. The fight at the lower end (under Custer) was not finished till near sunset.

Q. Did all the warriors leave the right and go to the left?

A. They did; the whole thing left.

Q. When Reno was driven across the creek, where was Sitting Bull?

A. I don't know.

Q. What were the families doing when the fighting was going on on the hill?

A. The women fled to the lower end of the camp and left everything.

Q. What did they do when they heard the firing on the left by Custer?

A. The upper end of the camp was at this time all deserted, and at the lower end of the camp they took down and packed the lodges ready for flight.

Q. I have heard that after the Custer fight, the Indians went back to the other end and attacked there again. How is it?

A. That is correct; the Indian soldiers went back and attacked the troops (Reno) on the hill again.

Q. Did you hear the firing?

A. Yes, I heard the firing while moving away.

It must be explained that Kill Eagle took the opportunity of the confusion to steal away from Sitting Bull's camp. His evidence shows that there was no design or trap on the part of the Indians, that they were really surprised, that Custer's attack was a second surprise, and that they were in the wildest confusion; this, too, when Reno's hesitating assault had convinced them that there was nothing to be feared from him. Now for Custer's fight. The trail shows that he came down to the ford, and was there driven back, leaving dead men and horses. The rest of the description is thus given by an officer of the general staff who examined the ground:

"From this point he was driven back to make successive stands on the higher ground. His line of retreat stretches from the river to the spot indicated on the map as that where he fell. On the line of retreat Calhoun's company seems to have been thrown across it to check the Indians. At a distance of about three-quarters of a mile from the river the whole of Calhoun's company lay dead, in an irregular line, Calhoun and Crittenden in place in the rear. About a mile beyond this, on the ridge parallel to

AUTIE REED.

BOSTON CUSTER

CAPT. CALHOUN

COL. TOM CUSTER.

the stream, still following the line of retreat indicated on the map, Keogh's company was slaughtered in position, his right resting on the hill where Custer fell, and which seems to have been held by Yates' company. On the most prominent point of this ridge Custer made his last desperate stand. Here, with Captain Yates, Colonel Cook, Captain Custer, Lieutenant Riley and others, and thirty-two men of Yates' command, he went down, fighting heroically to the last, against the tremendous odds which assailed them on all sides. It is believed by some that, finding the situation a desperate one, they killed their horses for a barricade. From the point where Custer fell the line of retreat again doubles back toward the river through a ravine, and along this line in the ravine twenty-three bodies of Smith's company were found. Where this line terminates near the river are found the dead men and horses of Captain Custer's company commingled with Smith's, and the situation of the dead indicates that some desperate attempt was made to make a stand near the river or to gain the woods."

There we have the short and simple history of the fight which was going on within two miles of Benteen and Reno for three long, weary hours. It is dry and simple in its words, but what a wealth of heroism that simple story reveals. This little band was made of Custer's men, under Custer's best officers, Custer's little knot of chosen friends. All we can do is to fill out its details. On this line, Calhoun's company was thrown across to check the Indians. The men lay dead in an irregular line, Calhoun and Crittenden in place in rear. This is the order of the tactics, the officers watching and moving along their line, within a few feet. There they fell, every man in his place. They were ordered to stay and be killed, to save the day, and they obeyed orders. Who, then, was Calhoun, that he was the first ordered to die?

Lieutenant James Calhoun, of the Seventh Cavalry, was the husband of Custer's only sister; he was Custer's dearest of all friends on earth; he was the bravest and gentlest of men, with the face and form of an Apollo, bright, fair hair and dark eyes, a man whom a lady who knew him well describes as the "handsomest man I ever saw." He was a gentleman's son, with all the education of a gentleman, and the most refined literary taste, who yet had not hesitated to enlist as a private soldier in the regular army, and had actually worked his way up, refined and sensitive as he was, in the midst of all the discomforts, hardships and degradations which surrounded the life of a private soldier at the close of the war, to a well-earned commission. He married Maggie E. Custer in Monroe, Michigan, March 7th, 1872, and acted as Custer's post adjutant during the time the regiment was divided. He was remarkably quiet and reserved in demeanor, but hid beneath his calm dignity of outward seeming the most lofty aspirations. Too young to have gained distinction in the Civil War, he hoped yet to gain it by unwavering fidelity to his duty. Duty was his one watchword, and by it he hoped to attain success. Such was the bright, brave youth whom Custer told to stay behind and be killed, so that the day might be saved. Did Calhoun murmur—did he question the order? Why did Custer leave him there to die?

Not a murmur came from the one, and the other showed by this his first sacrifice that he placed the country above all his earthly loves. "The country needs; I give her a man who will do his duty to the death: I give them my first brother. I leave my best loved sister a widow, that so the day may be saved. Farewell."

Well did Calhoun redeem that trust. Every man in his place, no faltering, no going back. Calhoun's company kept on firing till the last cartridge was gone, and one by one dropped dead in his tracks under the fire of the swarms of Indians that kept dashing to and fro before them, firing volley after volley. Down they went, one after another, cheered up by this grand figure of Duty, young Calhoun encouraging them to the last. With him young Crittenden, of the Twelfth Infantry, a mere boy, only appointed the previous fall, and temporarily with the cavalry in his first and last battle, as cool as his chief, cheered and steadied by the calm, princely dignity of courage that inspired that glorious stand. So they stood till the last man was down, and Crittenden was killed, and then came the friendly bullet that sent the soul of James Calhoun to an eternity of glory. Let no man say such a life was thrown away. The spectacle of so much courage must have nerved the whole command to the heroic resistance it made. Calhoun's men would never have died where they did, in line, had Calhoun not been there to cheer them. They would have been found in scattered groups, fleeing or huddled together, not fallen in their ranks, every man in his place, to the very last. Calhoun, with his forty men, had done on an open field what Reno, with a hundred and forty, could not do defending a wood. He had died like a hero, and America will remember him while she remembers heroes.

Let us go on with the tale. About a mile beyond, Keogh's company was slaughtered in position, his right resting on the hill where Custer fell. Custer had chosen the best ground to be found, and was determined to retreat no farther. By this time he must have realized that Reno had been beaten, but he trusted at least to Benteen to come and help him. The Indians were all around him, but a vigorous attack by Benteen on their rear would beat them, could Custer only hold them long enough.

Keogh was an older soldier than any there. He had been an officer in the Papal service in the days when Garibaldi made war upon the Holy Father, and he had served on the staffs of Buford and Stoneman during the war. The sight of Calhoun's men, dying as they did, had nerved Keogh's men to the same pitch of sublime heroism. Every man realized that it was his last fight, and was resolved to die game. Down they went, slaughtered in position, man after man dropping in his place, the survivors contracting their line to close the gaps. We read of such things in history, and call them exaggerations. The silent witness of those dead bodies of heroes in that mountain pass cannot lie. It tells plainer than words how they died, the Indians all around them, first pressing them from the river, then curling round Calhoun, now round Keogh, till the last stand on the hill by Custer, with three companies.

How that fight went, Curley, the Upsorako scout, tells us, he the only man who escaped alive, and who got away to the steamer Far West, lying at the mouth of the river. His testimony was taken by the officers of Terry's staff, through an interpreter. It is plain and prosaic in its simplicity, but it tells the tale.

He says he went down with two other Crows and went into action with Custer. "The General," he says, "kept down the river on the north bank four miles, after Reno had crossed to the south side above. He thought Reno would drive down the valley, so that they could attack the village on two sides, he believing Reno would take it at the upper end, while he (Custer) would go in at the lower end. Custer had to go farther down the river and farther away from Reno than he wished on account of the steep bank along the north side; but at last he found a ford and dashed for it. The Indians met him and poured in a heavy fire from across the narrow river. Custer dismounted to fight on foot, but could not get his skirmishers over the stream. Meantime, hundreds of Indians, on foot and on ponies, poured over the river, which was only about three feet deep, and filled the ravine on each side of Custer's men. Custer then fell back to some high ground behind him and seized the ravines in his immediate vicinity. The Indians completely surrounded Custer and poured in a terrible fire on all sides. They charged Custer on foot in vast numbers, but were again and again driven back. The fight began about 2 o'clock and lasted," Curly says, "almost until the sun went down over the hills. The men fought desperately, and, after the ammunition in their belts was exhausted, went to their saddlebags, got more and continued the fight. He also says the big chief (Custer) lived until nearly all his men had been killed or wounded, and went about encouraging his soldiers to fight on." Curly says when he saw Custer was hopelessly surrounded, he watched his opportunity, got a Sioux blanket, put it on, and worked up a ravine, and when the Sioux charged he got among them, and they did not know him from one of their own men. There were some mounted Sioux, and seeing one fall, Curly ran to him, mounted his pony, and galloped down as if going towards the white men, but went up a ravine and got away.

When questioned closely by one of the officers,* he mentioned one little fact about his escape that is pregnant with light on Custer's fate. When he saw that the party with the General was to be overwhelmed, he went to the General and begged him to let him show him a way to escape. General Custer dropped his head on his breast in thought for a moment, in a way he had of doing. There was a lull in the fight after a charge, the encircling Indians gathering for a fresh attack. In that moment, Custer looked at Curly, waved him away and rode back to the little group of men, to die with them. How many thoughts must have crossed that noble soul in that brief moment. There was no hope of victory if he stayed, nothing but certain death. With the scout he was nearly certain to escape. His horse was a thoroughbred and his way sure. He might have balanced the value of a leader's life against those of his men, and sought his safety. Why did he go back to certain death?

Because he felt that such a death as that which that little band of heroes was about to die was worth the lives of all the general officers in the world. Thanks to the story of the Crow scout, we know that he had the chance to live alone, and that he deliberately accepted death with his men as the worthier. He weighed, in that brief moment of reflection, all the consequences to America of the lesson of life and the lesson of heroic death, and he chose death. The Indian hovered around the fight, still watching; in the confusion he was not noticed, or taken for a Sioux. He had washed off his Upsaroka paint and let down his hair like a Sioux. Let us see what he saw.

Curly did not leave Custer until the battle was nearly over, and he describes it as desperate in the extreme. He is quite sure the Indians had more killed than Custer had white men with him.

There was the little group of men on the hill, the Indians hovering round them like hounds baying a lion, dashing up close and receding, the bullets flying like swarms of bees, the men in the

---

* This officer told the story personally to Mrs. Custer afterwards.

little group dropping one by one. At last the charm of Custer's charmed life was broken.

He got a shot in the left side and sat down, with his pistol in his hand. Another shot struck Custer and he fell over. The last officer killed was a man who rode a white horse (believed to be Lieut. Cook, adjutant of the Seventh, as Lieuts. Cook and Calhoun were the only officers who rode white horses, and Lieut. Calhoun was found dead on the skirmish line, near the ford, and probably fell early in the action).

At last they were all gone, every officer of the group. Custer fallen and Cook killed, the remaining men broke. Then the scout fled, too.

He says as he rode off he saw, when nearly a mile from the battlefield, a dozen or more soldiers in a ravine, fighting with Sioux all around them. He thinks all were killed, as they were outnumbered five to one, and apparently dismounted. These were no doubt part of the thirty-five missing men reported in the official dispatches of General Terry. Curly says he saw one cavalry soldier who had got away. He was well mounted, but shot through both hips, and Curly thinks he died of his wounds, starved to death in the bad lands, or more likely his trail was followed and he was killed by the Sioux.

Thirty-two men of Yates' company fell with their chief and the other officers on the hill; the rest of them, with Captain Custer's and Captain Smith's men, tried to cut their way to the river and all fell in the ravine. "Then," says Kill Eagle, "the Indian wounded came streaming back into Sitting Bull's camp, saying: "We have killed them all; put up your lodges where they are."

From the account of some Indians who went across the line into British America, to trade with the Manitoba Indians, we gain more particulars of the last fight than Curly could see. The scout was so utterly broken down with fear and agony of mind when he reached the steamer that he could not for a long time give a connected account, but his exultant enemies have filled the gap with their boasts. From these it appears that when only a few of the officers were left alive, the Indians made a hand-to-hand charge, in which Custer fought like a tiger with his sabre when his last shot was gone; that he killed or wounded three Indians with his sabre, and that as he ran the last man through, Rain-in-the-Face kept his oath and shot Custer.

While this account disagrees with that of Curly, I am inclined to believe it, for several reasons. Curly was some way off, the confusion was great, and the two brothers Custer were dressed alike and resembled each other closely in figure. I am inclined to believe that it was Colonel Tom Custer whom Curly saw fall as he described it. On the other hand, several Indians who were in the fight have told the same story about the sabre, and have given Big Rain or Rain-in-the-Face as the man who shot the General. We know Custer to have been a man of great strength and activity, one who had used the sabre freely in the Civil War; and in his last struggle such a man would have been as able to kill three Indians as was Shaw, the famous English guardsman at Waterloo, who was seen to kill nine French cuirassiers with his sword before he was shot. A last reason that is convincing is this: It is well known that the Indians did not mutilate Custer's body, it being the only one in that group entirely spared. The only reason for such a respect could have been a reverence for his valor. It is also well known that the Indians regard the striking of a living enemy with a hand weapon as the highest proof of valor possible, placing a very different estimate on shooting an enemy. All the reports of the Indians who reached the British possessions were unanimous in saying that they dreaded the sabre more than anything, and this is easily understood when their superstition as to hand weapons is considered. It seems certain that they would never have reverenced Custer's body as they did had he not struck down their best men in that grim hand-to-hand fight, wherein, among all the brave and strong, he was the bravest and best swordsman of all, the other officers having had but little teaching in the use of the sabre. Be that as it may, it is known that he must have died under circumstances of peculiar heroism to win such respect, and that he was only killed by the bravest Indian of the whole Northwest, a man whose unflinching fortitude had enabled him to hang in the air for four hours in the Sun Dance.

So fell Custer, the brave cavalier, the Christian soldier, surrounded by foes, but dying in harness amid the men he loved. Who fell with him?

There by his side lay his brother Tom, brave Colonel Custer, a double of the General, who had enlisted as a private soldier at 16, was an officer at 19, who wore what no other officer in the army could boast of, two medals, each for a flag taken from an enemy in battle. Brave and gentle, courteous and tender, a model officer of cavalry, God be with gallant Tom Custer till the last day. He died like all the Custers, with his face to the sky and his feet to the foe.

Not far off, close together, lay two more of the same family, poor young Boston Custer and little Autie Reed, Custer's nephew, son of that good, gentle Christian woman, who had saved Custer himself from a reckless career, whose prayers had helped to make him the Christian knight he became. Brave boys, nearly boys both, no sworn soldier of the state could die more nobly than they, who would not abandon a brother and kinsman. They could do little for him, but they could die with him. Autie was fresh from school a few weeks before, and wild to see the plains with "Uncle Autie." To take him along it was necessary to give him some official employment, and Custer, knowing that the rough, hard life would make a man of the boy, had him and another schoolmate appointed herders, to help drive the great herd of cattle with the column. Rough as the lot was, the lad never complained. He was seeing wild life, which was all he wanted, and had obtained leave to go on this scout with the General. Boston Custer's official position was that of forage master to the Seventh Cavalry, which he had held some time. He had been for years of a consumptive tendency, and his only chance for life was the open-air existence of the plains. How far better for him the wild, heroic death he died, under the blue sky, fighting like a true Custer, to the slow, lingering, failing end of a consumptive, which was his certain portion had he lived.

So closed the lives of the three Custers and their young nephew, fallen on that stricken field. It is time to turn to the comrades who fell with them.

There is something remarkable in the power which Custer apparently possessed of attracting to his side and intimate companionship the noblest and best of the men with whom the army brought him in contact; and the facts of his death bring out this power in a conspicuous manner. It is clear that when he made the division of the regiment into battalions in the morning, Custer knew that heavy work was coming, and intended to take the heaviest work into his own hands, as he always did. Into his own battalion he seems to have gathered all of his own familiar friends, including his three brothers, as knowing he could depend on them to the death. His confidence was well repaid, and we may say today, without fear of contradiction that Custer and Custer's friends were the flower of the Seventh Cavalry. The battalion that fell with Custer held them nearly all.

There was the Adjutant, Brevet-Colonel Wm. W. Cook, the last officer left living, and whose final fall broke the hearts of his men and ended the battle. Cook was a model of manly beauty, in a very different style from that of Calhoun. Fully as tall (both were over six feet), and as powerfully framed, Cook was the image of a typical English Life Guardsman, with his high-bred aristocratic features and long, wavy black moustache and whiskers. Like Keogh, he was a foreigner, having been born in Canada, whence he entered the American service in the Twenty-fourth

New York Cavalry, rising to its colonelcy. The reader has seen his name frequently during Custer's life on the plains. One proud sentence will be his best epitaph. In choosing an officer to command the sharpshooters of the Seventh Cavalry in the Washita campaign, the question was not, says Custer, "to choose a good one, but among many good to choose the best." He chose Cook. Let it be written: "Custer said he was his best officer."

By his side was gallant Yates, captain and brevet-colonel, tender and true, a man like Calhoun, of old family and gentle blood, who had not hesitated to enter the ranks as a soldier in the war, had enlisted as a boy of sixteen and worked his way up to a captaincy in the Regular Army. Yates was a true, sterling fellow, a soldier to the backbone, with the crack company of the Seventh. They used to call his troop the "band-box troop," so neat were they always, with an affectation of military dandyism. It was a tradition in that company that every man who died from it, "died with his boots on," the homely western phrase that tells such a story of unflinching courage. There fell brave old Yates, game to the last, with every man of the little "band-box troop" in his place, round their leader, who fell with a smile on his lips. He and they had done their duty, and died like men. God will help the widow and fatherless.

The last company commander of all fell near Yates, Lieutenant and Brevet-Captain Algernon E. Smith, one more member of that little circle of refined, quiet gentlemen who had shared Custer's friendship at Fort Lincoln. Captain Smith was one of the bravest and most modest of men. One little incident will illustrate his character better than a volume of description. During the Civil War, while a captain of volunteers, Captain Smith was detailed on the staff of General Terry, at that desperate storming of Fort Fisher which gave Terry his star in the Regular Army. During the storming, a regiment faltered under the tremendous fire, having lost two color-bearers and all its field officers. Smith seized the colors, led on the regiment, sprang on the parapet and was among the first in the works, where he fell severely wounded, his left shoulder smashed by a musket ball. For this he was brevetted major of volunteers. The wound healed, but in such a manner that he could never after lift his left arm above the shoulder. He was appointed to the Seventh Cavalry in 1867 and served in every campaign, in familiar intercourse with his brother officers; yet very few in the regiment ever knew he had served in the Civil War, and none of the ladies would have known that he had been wounded, but for an accidental remark by his wife in 1875, from which it came out that he could not put on his uniform without assistance on account of his crippled left arm. Algernon Smith died as he had lived, a simple, modest soldier, in front of his men; while behind him lay the twenty-three bodies of the poor disheartened remnant that tried to cut their way out, when all was over and their beloved officer killed.

And now we come to the last of all, the youngest of that little band, Lieutenant William Van W. Reily. His portrait lies before me as these words are written, and it is hard to keep the cold composure of the impartial chronicler as I think of his peculiarly touching history. His father, a gallant officer of the U. S. Navy, went down in his ship in the Indian Ocean, and not a soul came back to tell the tale, before Reily was born. That father sailed away from a bride of a few months never to return, and his boy left the mother who idolized him, to meet a similar fate, amid foes as pitiless as the ocean waves. Willie Reily fell next to Custer, and his fair young body was found lying at the feet of his commander. A good, noble-looking face he had, with a certain wistful, musing expression, prophetic of his early fate. He had been ill for some time before the expedition started, and the surgeon wished to order him on some post duty, but he refused to stay, and was eager to share the fate of his regiment, whatever it might be. He had his dearest wish; he died like his brave father, at his post doing his duty. Let no man say such an end was sad: it was heroic. We must all die sometime, but not all like him. To him and all such, America says, "God bless our brave dead."

CHAPTER VII

I have told the facts of Custer's last battle as closely as the means at hand will permit the truth to be ascertained. Beginning my task with a strong impression, produced by the official reports, that Custer had been rash and imprudent, and that the conduct of Reno and Benteen had been that of prudent and brave soldiers, a careful examination of all the accessible evidence has left me no other course than to tell the whole story, to vindicate the reputation of a noble man from unjust aspersions. I leave the facts to the world to judge whether I am not right in these conclusions—

1. Had Reno fought as Custer fought, and had Benteen obeyed Custer's orders, the battle of the Little Big Horn might have proved Custer's last and greatest Indian victory.

It may be objected to this conclusion that the numbers of the Indians were too great to admit it: but a careful examination of the conflicting statements leads to the belief that these numbers have been exaggerated by Reno in his report, to cover his own conduct. He estimates the Indians at 3,500 "at the least," and the popular impression has since increased this estimate anywhere up to ten thousand. Herndon, the scout, a much cooler person, puts them at only 2,000 or 2,500; and Benteen thinks they were only 900. One means of approximate computation is unwittingly offered by Reno. Near the close of his report he mentions the whole village as defiling away before his eyes, and says "The length of the column was fully equal to that of a large division of the cavalry corps of the Army of the Potomac, as I have seen it on the march." The divisions of the Cavalry Corps, at their strongest, were about 4,000 men; and they had no women and children with them. Making the very smallest allowance for led horses, pack horses, squaws and children, it is clear that at least one-half of the column must be taken away to leave the true number of warriors. This would give us 2,000, and if we allow 500 for the losses in fighting Reno and Custer, we come to Herndon's estimate. These numbers were four to one of Custer's, but he had fought such odds before, at the Washita, and came out triumphant. The obstinacy of his attack shows that he expected to conquer. He could have run like Reno had he wished, and Reno says in the report he thought Custer had done so. It is clear, in the light of Custer's previous character, that he held on to the last, expecting to be supported, as he had a right to expect. It was only when he clearly saw he had been betrayed that he resolved to die game, as it was then too late to retreat.

2.   Had not President Grant, moved by private revenge, displaced Custer from command of the Fort Lincoln column, Custer would be alive today and the Indian war settled.

The Dakota column would have been confided to the best Indian-fighter of the army; Reno and Benteen would never have dreamed of disobeying their chief, had they not known he was out of favor at court; Custer and Gibbon would have cooperated as men both familiar with Indian warfare, and cross-purposes would have been avoided.

The action of a court of inquiry, which will be able to call forth the testimony of officers whose names the author withholds from the public at present, will settle whether these conclusions are correct or not. Many witnesses have been deterred from speaking by fear of those superiors whom their evidence will impeach; and these witnesses will be able to swear in public to what they have hitherto only dared to say and write in private. The nation demands such a court, to vindicate the name of a dead hero from the pitiless malignity, which first slew him and then pursued him beyond the grave.

CHAPTER VIII

CUSTER, THE SOLDIER.

The popular idea of Custer as a soldier is that of a brave, reckless, dashing trooper, always ready to charge any odds, without knowing or caring what was the strength of his enemy, and trusting to luck to get out of his scrapes. In the public mind, he has always been associated, even by his admirers, with Murat and Prince Rupert, as a type of mere impetuosity.

A great deal of this impression among civilians has been the effect, partly of the frequency of his dashing personal exploits, but very largely also to a combination of the sneers of professional soldiers envious of his fame, and of the anxiety of the war correspondents to write home a "picturesque" letter. During the Civil War the so-called war correspondents seldom knew much of military life, and had rarely been soldiers before that war. As a consequence, they wrote home a great many rediculous stories about Custer, the product of camp gossip. He was accused of putting his hair up in papers, of wearing stays, using curling tongs, etc., and the ingenious correspondent of one New York paper set the seal on the whole by a stilted account of the runaway of Don Juan and Custer at the last parade. He thus became, to a large part of the public, a perfectly ideal personage, as unlike the real Custer as Tom Moore's poetry was unlike the real quiet, domestic Tom Moore.

The real Custer was as far from being the reckless harumscarum cavalier of public fancy as possible. He was a remarkably quiet, thoughtful man, when any work was on hand, one who never became flurried and excited in the hottest battle, and who, on a campaign, was a model of wary watchfulness, a man who was never surprised during his whole career, and who was equal to any emergency of whatever kind.

Three times during Custer's service as a brigade commander, did he find himself surrounded by enemies and compelled to cut his way through, and on none of those three occasions could the slightest blame be attached to him for the dilemma. The first time was at Brandy Station, and there the fault was that of Meade or Pleasonton, who had divided their cavalry forces, so that when the separate units came together the enemy was between them. The second time was at Buckland's Mills, where the disaster was due entirely to Kilpatrick's headlong rashness after he had been warned of his danger by the wary Custer. The third time was at Trevillian Station, in 1864. There, his danger was due to the accidental direction of a force of the enemy, driven in by Custer's friends from another direction. It was, in fact, Brandy Station reversed.

As a division commander, having no one else to trouble him, being responsible for his own actions, he was never in the slightest difficulty, and this is true of his whole after career. Put Custer in chief command, and he never made a mistake: put him under any one else, except Sheridan, as perfect a soldier as himself, and he was always suffering for the blunders, mistakes, or faint-heartedness of others, either his superiors or coadjutors.

The consequence was, to both Custer and Sheridan, the envy and detraction of all those who could not understand their peculiar quality of instant and correct decision under fire, as to the right thing to do. This faculty is given to very few indeed. In the Army of the Potomac, Custer and Sheridan were its only possessors, in the highest degree, the degree possessed by such men as Napoleon, Cromwell, Gustavus Adolphus, Caesar and Hannibal. It made them both supreme as "battle commanders," whatever their merits as strategists. Their detractors, who could not understand this faculty, tried to belittle it by setting down Sheridan as a "mere trooper," Custer as a reckless rider and fighter, a harum-scarum light dragoon.

In Custer's case, the prejudices of those who did not know him, invariably preceded his entrance on any new command, as invariably to be replaced by a feeling akin to adoration, from all who served under him, if they possessed any nobility and generosity of character. To dislike him was the infallible result either of want of personal knowledge, which was innocent, or of some meanness of character, with which Custer's impulsive generosity clashed. Of his first appearance in the Third Cavalry Division, General (then Colonel) A. B. Nettleton, commander of the "Fighting Second Ohio," thus speaks:

"I had never seen General Custer prior to his promotion to the command of our division, but he was well known to us by repute. Some of us were at first disposed to regard him as an adventurer, a disposition which a sight of his peculiar dress and long locks tended to confirm. One engagement with the enemy under Custer's leadership dissipated all these impressions, and gave our new commander his proper place. Once under fire, we found that a master hand was at the helm, that beneath the golden curls and broad-brimmed hat was a cool brain and a level head."

One thing that characterized Custer was this: having measured as accurately as possible the strength and morale of his enemy, and having made his own disposition of troops carefully and personally, he went into every fight with complete confidence in the ability of his division to do the work marked out for it. Custer's conduct in battle was characteristic. He never ordered his men to go where he would not lead, and he never led where he did not expect his men to follow. He probably shared with the private soldier the danger of the skirmish line oftener than any officer of his rank, not from wantonness of courage, but with a well-defined purpose on each occasion. He knew that the moral effect of his personal presence at a critical moment, was equal to a reinforcement of troops when a reinforcement could not be found.

A large part of Custer's success was due to the fact that he was a good pursuer. Unlike many equally brave and skillful officers, he was rarely content to hold a position or drive his enemy; he always gathered the fruit, as well as shook the tree of battle. He regarded his real work as only beginning, when the enemy was broken and flying.

Although his special forte was the command of cavalry in the field, he was not deficient in camp. He was a good disciplinarian, without being a martinet; particularly thorough in maintaining an effective picket line or outpost service, on which depends the safety of any army in quarters. By unexpected visits to the outposts by day and night, he personally tested the faithfulness and alertness of officers and men on picket duty. On more than one occasion I have known him to take the trouble to write a letter of commendation to the commander of the regiment on the picket line, praising the manner in which the duty was performed. There was nothing of the military scold in his nature. By timely praise, oftener than by harsh criticism, he stimulated his subordinates to fidelity, watchfulness and gallantry.

General Nettleton is quite competent to give an opinion of Custer, for he served under him with the most distinguished gallantry; and his regiment, the Second Ohio Cavalry, won this official praise from their division commander, in a letter to Governor Brough of Ohio: "I assure your excellency that in my entire division of twelve regiments from various States, there is not one on which I rely more implicitly than on the gallant Second. I have known it repeatedly to hold its place against terrible odds, when almost any other regiment would have felt warranted in retiring."

Of Nettleton, himself, he says: "I regard him as one of the most valuable officers in the service, and do not know his superior in the army as regards the qualities needed in a good cavalry commander."

We quote these words to show that in Nettleton a perfectly competent critic is found, as well as one possessing personal knowledge of Custer. His testimony is merely the echo of that of every officer of capacity who ever served under that general.

Some may think that in all this too much is claimed for our hero; but this verdict can only be given by those who have not examined the evidence on which the estimate is founded. As an army commander like Sheridan, as a corps commander, there are no means of estimating his powers, for he never had an opportunity of exhibiting them. As a cavalry officer, pure and simple, the most carping criticism can find no flaw in Custer's career, from the day he led the Michigan Brigade into the battle of Gettysburg to that in which he fell, fighting like a lion bayed by the hunters, deserted by his supporting detachments. He was, in fact, as nearly perfect as a cavalry commander can be.

Viewed from the standpoint of Seydlitz and the Great Frederick, and that at present prevailing in Europe, the actions of Custer are faultless, as far as he himself is concerned. The only wrong feature pervading them is one which was the fault of the system in which American cavalry has always been trained, and which even Custer could not remedy entirely, though he did his utmost towards checking it. This was the undue dependence of the men and officers on their firearms, and their reluctance to use the sabre. This fault Custer constantly strove against, and during his valley campaigns succeeded in forcing his men by personal example into charging with the sabre, with invariable success whenever it was employed. We must, however, for the truth's sake, undeceive the civilian reader who imagines that the sabre was the exclusive weapon used in any of the so-called "sabre charges," either of Custer's or any other cavalry command, during the war. A rattling, irregular fusillade of pistol and carbine shots almost invariably accompanied the charge, and, as a rule, the men were very poor swordsmen, solely from want of fencing practice.

Since the war, the case has been still worse, the use of the sabre having been practically abolished; and the diminished power of Custer, reduced as he was from a general to a field officer, added to the fact that he found the sense of his brother officers generally against him on this point, prevented his giving the queen of cavalry weapons that attention which it deserved.

But as a cavalry leader, Custer displayed more genius and natural talent than any officer in the American army; genius, moreover, of a kind that would have raised him to eminence in any service. Had Custer, with the same natural talent, served in the Franco-Prussian war as an officer of Uhlans, there is little or no doubt that he would have risen to higher command than he attained in our own service. The well-known personal supervision of Von Moltke, which has made the Prussian army what it is, by promotions for merit alone, would never have passed by Custer, with his wonderful faculty of seizing the moment and its fleeting opportunity.

The best cavalry leader America has ever produced is the only truthful verdict that experience can pass on him; a great cavalry leader for any time or country, history will finally pronounce him; worthy to stand beside Hannibal's "thunderbolt" Mago; Saladin, the leader of those "hurricanes of horse" that swept the Crusaders from Palestine; Cromwell, Seydlitz or Zieten; a perfect general of horse.

CHAPTER IX

CUSTER, THE INDIAN FIGHTER

If we devote a separate chapter to the consideration of Custer as an Indian campaigner, it is not because we deem that any different grade of talent is required for fighting Indians other than that which obtains in a contest with a civilized foe, but rather as a concession to the popular idea that such is the case. This idea is partly due to the natural propensity of "old Indian fighters" to magnify their own office, but also to the equally common tendency of mankind in general to ignore talent and special genius as a possible factor of success in any pursuit, making experience and age the only tests of competency. A comparison of results obtained in both kinds of warfare will give strong reason to believe that Indian fighting, the same as Arab fighting in Algeria, is by no means as difficult to master as the art of fighting a properly equipped, civilized foe. Many an officer who has attained considerable success as an Indian fighter has turned out but a poor general in campaign against a regular enemy, whereas generals of remarkable talent in civilized warfare—real generals, not mere "scientific soldiers," so miscalled—have never failed to give a good account of a barbarian foe, be it Indian, Arab, African or Tartar.

The natural tendency above referred to has, however, produced in the American army a very exaggerated estimate of the necessity of long experience in Indian fighting to produce a perfect officer, and a fashion of depreciating every officer, no matter what his talent elsewhere, if his Indian experience be brief. When Custer first went on the plains he found this feeling in full force, and was constantly confronted with the express or implied statement that Indian fighting was so totally different from other warfare that his previous experience was valueless, and that he would have to sit humbly and learn at the feet of this or that officer, because the latter was "an old Indian fighter."

Very early in his Indian career, however, Custer seems to have discovered that few army officers were able to supply him with much valuable information on the Indian subject; and his keen perception showed him at the same time who could do it. He saw that the officers, especially the oldest of them, were too slow for him, just as they had been during the war, and he also saw that the rough and ready scouts, who lived in the same style as the Indians, would be his best masters. From them he seems from the first to have taken lessons, readily and humbly enough, as he tells us in his recorded experiences on the plains. His first master was Comstock, the scout who rode with him in his first campaign against Pawnee Killer; and Pawnee Killer himself, with Romeo and California Joe, gave him excellent lessons. When we consider that Custer made his first appearance on the plains the beginning of April, 1867, perfectly "green," as the old Indian fighters thought; that the whole of his experience was limited to the months of April, May, June and a few days of July in that year; that from that time till September, 1868, he was under arrest and suspended from field service, it will appear that he must have used his time well to have called forth from his superior officers the request that met him in Monroe in 1868. His Indian fighting experience was then limited to less than four months; there was a whole army to choose from; the officers of the Seventh Cavalry had all been out on the plains a whole year; General Sully, an Indian fighter then possessing a high reputation, was in command; yet, such was the confidence in Custer's ability, produced by his record of three months and a half, that Sherman, Sheridan, Sully and all the officers of the regiment, old and new, joined in a request to have Custer back for the command of the field expedition.

He came, and what was the result? In six months he had pacified the whole of the southwestern tribes, first by battle, then by diplomacy, exhibiting throughout the campaign a combination of boldness and dexterity, of tact and shrewdness, that was crowned with complete success, and that stamped him as the best Indian fighter in the service. Measured by his deeds and comparing them with those of any Indian fighter in the service, no matter what his reputation, this claim is by no means extravagant. The exploits of those officers who fought Indians before the Civil War were not attended with the same difficulties which surrounded

Custer and the Indian fighters of the present day. In those days the troops were better armed than the Indians; now the Indians are better armed than the troops; then there was no Indian Department to feed the Indians and supply them with patent ammunition; now this business has become recognized as the regular employment of an Indian agent. In the old times the army was left alone to manage the Indians, to fight them if necessary, and Indian wars were easily settled on the plains; now the army officer has to fight the Indians first and the Indian Department afterwards. All these things made Custer's task a much harder one than those of the officers who engaged in an occasional Indian skirmish before the Civil War. With the services of any recent Indian campaigner, no matter who or what he may be, Custer's record need fear no comparison. The results of his campaign of 1868-9, when he was in full and unrestricted command, were superior to those gained by any other officer in the service, since 1866, and nothing but prejudice can gainsay the undoubted facts.

What was it, then, that gave Custer his remarkable success as an Indian fighter, after such a brief experience, and what were the qualities which, so early in his career, gained him the implicit confidence, not of Sheridan—which was his already—but of Sherman, who had only met him a few times; of Sully, who had not seen him at all in service? It was his remarkable tact, shrewdness, and quickness to learn, the ardor with which he applied himself to the study of the Indian character, and the safety which had accompanied his most apparently audacious operations against the enemy, in his three months' service. Besides this, when under arrest and suspension, Custer had not been idle. He had made up his mind to master the problem of Indian character, and he devoted his enforced leisure to the task. Where another man would have been brooding, Custer was working, and he devoted his winter of disgrace at Fort Leavenworth—to what, think you?— to learning the Indian sign language, which passed current among all the tribes, and serves as a medium of communication between Indians speaking every variety of language. This he studied to such good purpose, then and after, that he was able to converse, without an interpreter, with Indians of any tribe, as far as the sign language carries any of them.

That old Indian fighters in those days appreciated his knowledge of Indian character is evinced by the words of General Sturgis, himself an old ante-bellum Indian fighter of considerable reputation, which words we have quoted elsewhere. Custer, quick to learn Indian tactics, was equally quick to learn the habits and natures, peaceful and warlike, of the Indians themselves. An amusing anecdote, whose authenticity is vouched for, will show the tact and shrewdness with which he played on every point in Indian character.

While in camp on the Black Hills expedition, in 1873, being then in the zenith of his reputation as an Indian fighter, Custer retained a great many of his Indian scouts near headquarters, unler command of Bloody Knife. One day, as Custer was writing in his tent, one of these Indian scouts came in, a good deal the worse for liquor, and began some maundering complaint of something that had offended him. Custer looked up, saw the man was drunk, and ordered him out of the tent. Like all Indians in liquor, this one was insolent, and squaring himself before the General, became louder in his complaints and boasts of his importance.

Without another word, Custer sprang up, with the peculiar, cat-like agility he possessed, and, quick as lightning, struck the Indian two blows, in regular professional style, sending him to grass, with an ugly lump under the eye and a nose badly punished. The Indian was knocked half out of the tent door, and as Custer made a step towards him, as if to renew the assault, the red man picked himself up with surprising humility and ran like a deer to the scouts' quarters, howling all the way.

Custer returned to his writing as if nothing had happened. Very few men possessed the physique to have punished a powerful Indian so quickly, but Custer's knuckles were very bony, and from a lad he had been the strongest of his playmates. So far he had done nothing but what any powerful man of quick decision would have done. It is the sequel of the story which shows his tact.

In a few minutes after there was a great commotion in the Indian quarters, and the voices of the warriors could be heard, all together, in the high monotonous scream of the excited Indian, trying to lash himself and fellows to fury. It brought out the guard in some alarm, and the other soldiers began to tumble out of their tents to see the fun. Custer, of course, heard the disturbance and knew the cause, but he continued tranquilly writing, as if deafness had suddenly afflicted him. The noise increased, and he could hear the stern tones of the officer of the day in the wrangle, but even that dreaded official's authority did not appear to cow the Indians, for their fierce chattering grew shriller every moment. He heard in the hubbub the English words "Guardhouse, guardhouse, big chief—guardhouse," and a smile gathered over his face as he went on writing.

Presently a sudden hush came on the tumult. He heard steps approaching and a knock on the tent door, followed by the entrance of the officer of the day, who wore a countenance of some anxiety.

It appeared from the officer's report that the Indians were insisting that the same measure of justice should be meted to Custer as to other offenders. They had been accustomed to see every man found fighting in camp put in the guardhouse. The big chief had hurt their comrade badly, therefore the big chief ought to go to the guardhouse. While we cannot help smiling at the idea, it must be admitted that the rude sense of justice of the Indians was perfectly correct. The officer of the day further stated that he had pacified them by coming to see the big chief, but that they were very firm in their demands.

It may be imagined by some that there was no great difficulty in this case, but the contrary is the fact. If Custer had allowed the first Indian to be drunk and insolent, he would have lost control over his capricious allies, who would have despised him. If he now refused them justice they all would leave him, probably to join the hostiles. Custer's decision was instantly taken, though not in words.

As soon as the officer had concluded his report, the General walked out of the tent and found his Indian allies in a group, quite silent now, watching the tent. "Tell the chief to come here," said Custer to the officer of the day. In a few moments Bloody Knife approached, in a very lordly manner. As he left his comrades, he waved them back, with the grand air of a "big Injun" full of his own importance.

Custer approached the chief several steps to meet him, took off his hat, and swept a low and ceremonious salute. Then shaking Bloody Knife's hand cordially, he and the Indian mutually ejaculated "How, how." Still retaining the chief's haid, he led him into his own tent, and seated him in his own chair, an honor that gratified Bloody Knife still more.

Then the General took up an Indian pipe, filled it, lighted it, took a few whiffs, and handed it to the chief, the two sitting opposite to each other in solemn silence all the while. By this time the Indian was swelling with importance, and evidently imagined that the white chief was about to apologize and offer presents to pay for the wrong he had done. He behaved, however, with the strictest decorum, as an Indian generally does at a council. After several mutual whiffs, Custer gravely asked what had procured him the honor of this visit.

Thus exhorted, Bloody Knife, in broken English, uttered his complaint with ceremonious gravity. "Big chief hurt Injun heap bad—near kill um—cut face open—Injun much heap mad—say big chief must go guardhouse." And the chief grunted and re-lapsed into silence, smoking vigorously.

"Is your man badly hurt?" asked Custer, after the usual pause of ceremony.

"Much heap bad—face all blood—maybe die—Injuns put um in bed—tink he die—say big chief must go guardhouse." And he grunted a second time, feeling that he had made a point, then ceremoniously handed the pipe to Custer. The fact probably was he was waiting to be bribed.

After a minute's pause, Custer spoke very gravely. "Listen. I am the big chief here. All these soldiers are under me, and all their chiefs, too. You see that?" The chief bowed gravely, and grunted. "You are the chief of the scouts. All the Indians are under you, because you are a great warrior. You see?" A more decided grunt of approbation and gratified vanity. "Whenever any of my soldiers has a complaint, he goes to his chief, and his chief comes to me. You see?" A sort of doubtful grunt. The Indian began to see that something else was coming. "No one ever enters this tent but chiefs and great warriors. Them I am always glad to see. You I am glad to see. You are a chief, and a great warrior. You see?" The grunt this time was one of un-mixed satisfaction. "When a man comes into my tent without first going to his chief," pursued Custer slowly, watching his auditor closely, "he dishonors his chief—you see?—makes a squaw of his chief—you see?—throws dirt in his chief's face—you see?—says 'You are no chief—you are a squaw—a dog'—do you see?"

In his turn, Custer resumed the puffing of his pipe, which he had interrupted to speak. For fully a minute there was a dead silence. Then the chief rose, and Custer laid aside the pipe and followed suit. Not being a smoker, he was only too glad to do it. The chief shook his hand ceremoniously. "How, how," said he. Then, suddenly dropping his dignity, he shot out of the tent toward the Indian quarters, and a moment later Custer heard his voice raised in a perfect frenzy of rage, yelling out an impas-sioned appeal to his followers to avenge him on the man who had made a squaw of so great a chief as Bloody Knife, the Arickaree.

A few moments later all the Indians rushed to the quarters where the poor sufferer was in bed, nursed by his friends, pulled him out, and commenced lashing him with their heavy buffalo whips, the chief being the heaviest in his blows. The innate sense of the necessity of subordination in military society was aroused. Even the wild savage could see the force of Custer's lucid argument, though delivered in a strange language, and with some words only half understood.*

Custer had no more trouble with his Indian scouts, and he showed the same knowledge of Indian character throughout his career. The story of Rain-in-the-Face partly illustrates it, but there are enough anecdotes of the kind to fill a book much larger than this, which cannot now be told. In the Southwest and Northwest alike, when the outside world deemed that Custer was merely stagnating in ordinary army style, he was carrying on his study of Indian character, and acquiring ascendency and reputation among the tribes. In his visits to New York, he took occasion to learn a good many feats of conjuring, sleight-of-hand, etc., which he used in various adroit ways to increase this ascendency; so that, at the time of his death, he had the reputation among the Indians of being a great magician or "medicine man," which increased the awe with which they regarded him. That, and his superhuman courage, which Indians, of all men, are the first to respect, procured him the last honor which they could pay to his mortal remains. They dared to kill him from afar with bullets; that was merely the crooking of a finger, but something in that dead body struck even Rain-in-the-Face with a sense of awe, and the bravest Sioux of the Northwest did not dare to lift his hand to strike dead Custer.

Will any be found to take his place and do as well as he has done? It is hard to say. So far, the American army has produced but one Custer, and it is doubtful whether the peculiar combination of qualities which made him what he was will ever be duplicated. If one be found to lead men to success as he has done, he must be looked for among the younger officers of the army, the men whose careers are yet to culminate, who show symptoms of life amid the too general stagnation of frontier service.

Two at least of this class, the hope of the army of the future, have developed talents of the same nature as those of Custer, and which may in time equal them in degree. To them the country looks to give it a successor to Custer, the Indian fighter, in quickness of resolution, impetuosity of attack, sagacity of plan. One of them, since the greater part of these pages were written, has gained the only success of a disastrous campaign by meeting Sitting Bull on open ground, and, aided by artillery, repulsing his attack with severe loss; the other, by his now nearly forgotten

---

* A partial version of this anecdote first appeared in the Chicago Inter-Ocean, and subsequent investigation by the author has resulted in the above facts. Poor Bloody Knife fell with Custer at the Little Horn.

raid over the Mexican border, showed the possession of just such boldness and enterprise as were conspicuous in Custer; and to Miles and Mackenzie the army looks to give them another successful Indian fighter, a man not afraid of the Indians, but fighting as if he expected a victory.

But, as we have before this insisted on, the greatest reform necessary in the present regular cavalry, to make it uniformly effective against Indians, is in the instruction of the rank and file, and especially in the cultivation of that neglected weapon, the sabre, to raise the morale of the force. As it is, it takes more than ordinary bravery and conduct in any officer to achieve success with the half-trained recruits that form the main body of the frontier army; and the disuse of the sabre has turned the once brave American dragoon into a timid skirmisher, who shrinks from the shock of the levelled lance, and seeks safety in infantry tactics.

CHAPTER X

CUSTER, THE MAN

If the readers of this book have not by this time formed some idea of the character of Custer as a man, the labors of the author have been spent in vain, and it would be useless to write further. Still, inasmuch as the beautiful family and social life of our hero has not been fully treated of elsewhere, we have judged it best to say here a few words on the subject, to complete the picture.

In society, apart from these occasional moody intervals, he was exceedingly light-hearted, with a boyish tendency to frolic and playfulness that seemed common to all the Custer boys. In Fort Lincoln, where he was thrown almost alone during the winter into a very small circle of intimate friends, he and his brothers, Tom and Boston, were the life of the place, while the refining influence of the society of the few ladies that clustered around Mrs. Custer made the circle extremely deilghtful. No man valued more highly than Custer the influence of women to ameliorate men, and no man had more reason. The little group of ladies, Mrs. Custer, Mrs. Calhoun, Mrs. Yates, Mrs. Smith, and the one or two young ladies from Monroe who were always visiting Mrs. Custer, made the home circle at the fort a perfect haven of rest to the officers fortunate enough to possess Custer's friendship.

The General was always very fond of children. One of his Eastern friends, whom he frequently visited, tells how he would often leave a circle of fashionable people, with whom he was very shy and reserved, to sit in a corner with two children, who begged him for Indian stories. Although very reticent to others about his deeds, he always unbent to these children, and so won their hearts that today they always protest that General Custer was the kindest and nicest gentleman that ever visited their father's house. I set a high value on this fact. Children, especially girls, are unerring readers of character, and there must have been something singularly pure and frank in Custer's character to have attracted the love of these children.

Another point in Custer was his perfect nobility of forgiveness. We have seen how his court-martial in 1867 was caused by an officer, brave and capable enough, but who hated him. Only a year later, this same officer, then out of the service, applied to Custer for a position as trader or sutler in an expedition commanded by him, expressing his sorrow for the past. Custer at once gave him the place, which was in his gift. Yet his critics have called him "a good friend and a bitter enemy." Never was a falser saying. The man seemed incapable of private malice. Even under the unjust persecution of Grant he was cheerful, and always said to those who spoke bitterly of the President, "Never mind; it will all come right at last. The President is mistaken; but it will all come right at last, if I do my duty." He was never known to return an injury.

In his devotion to duty and honesty, to fair dealing and justice, he was almost fanatical. There, indeed, he was stern, and his indignation at the robbery and rapacity of the Indian ring and the post traders' ring was frequent and outspoken. It caused all his subsequent trouble. He saw the poor agency Indians robbed while the agents grew rich, and his anger, which could not find vent through official channels, was heard in the press, and given to the world in his "Life on the Plains." Can we blame him for that?

Custer knew, as every officer in the army knows, that the Indian Department is a perfect mine of wealth to the men of politics, and that, were it not for the supplies of arms furnished to the Indians by that department, there would be no Indian wars. He and his men were finally shot to death with bullets loaded into Winchester metallic ammunition at New Haven and Bridgeport, Connecticut, and furnished to the Indians by the Indian Bureau. He knew that in every fight he had with Indians they confronted him with weapons sold them by traders under the protection of the agencies. He knew that every attempt by honest men in Congress to abolish this grand corruption mine had been defeated by the vote of a purchased majority. He knew that the reason for this vote was the enormous amount of power given by the use of such a huge corruption fund for political purposes. He knew that the very arms sold to hostile Indians were made a means of cheating them, so that a single Winchester rifle, worth thirty dollars, sold for two hundred buffalo robes at Fort Peck. He saw all these soulless cheats around him bartering away the lives of the frontier settlers by the hundred for their gain, and he groaned in spirit, and spoke out again and again, in fiery anger, against such monstrous wrongs. Can we blame him?

His one fault, to the sense of cool, selfish men of the world, was his outspoken frankness, his anger at wrong, his want of concealment. Make the most of that, and it is a noble fault. It brought him his death.

Truth and sincerity, honor and bravery, tenderness and sympathy, unassuming piety and temperance, were the mainspring of Custer, the man. As a soldier there is no spot on his armor; as a man no taint on his honor.

We have followed him through all his life, and passed in review boy, cadet, lieutenant, captain, general, and Indian fighter, without finding one deed to bring shame on soldier or man. People of the land he loved, my task is ended. Would it had been committed to worthier hands. Four simple lines, written by an unknown poet, form his best epitaph:

"Who early thus upon the field of glory
    Like thee doth fall and die, needs for his fame
Naught but the simple telling of his story,
    The naming of his name."

CHAPTER XI

George Armstrong Custer was of that great industrial class from which so many of our original men are springing. With no marked advantages of education, no influence to push forward his fortunes, or wealth to command situation, he yet passed through such a career, was so rapid in growth and development, that he was ripe in honors when the bullet of the Indian warrior pierced his heart. Advancement so swift, a career so brilliant, that his deeds have become household words in the land, indicate the possession of more than ordinary qualities in the subject of this memoir. Leaving, at barely his majority, the military academy where his original address and marked demeanor had placed him, without the usual influence which peoples our national training schools, he was thrust at once into a command at the outbreak of the war. Having barely reached a man's estate, unused to the world, unacquainted with men, untrained in active warfare, he was suddenly to be called upon for the exhibition of the qualities which lead and govern armies. The sword of the cadet was to be unsheathed by youthful hands amidst the din of a civil strife, unexampled in history for the fierceness of its character and for the importance of its results. Out of this trial our hero was to emerge covered with the glory of a veteran, decorated, after five years of service, at the age of 26, with the stars of a Major General, and renowned from one end of the country to the other —throughout the world, indeed,—as an original and brilliant fighter, a bold and dashing soldier, a successful commander. The greater part of his career, so sadly terminated, was passed where the fight raged hottest, where death and carnage reigned supreme; and finally, at the age of 37, an age when the careers of most men are beginning, he was snatched away, covered with glory, the mourned darling of a nation. We must look into the records of heroic ages for a parallel to this career, through which our biographer has so lovingly followed him. The incidents of that extraordinary military history can be followed and proven in the annals of the war. Dates and official records will amply note and verify the conspicuous part borne by General Custer. His place among the heroes of our country will be gratefully allowed so long as patriotism endures; his chivalrous deeds will be immortalized by bard and perpetuated by historian. The chapter of great warriors will hereafter be incomplete which does not record the exploits of Custer and his gallant riders, from Bull Run to Appomattox.

It is the misfortune of men in high public station that the brilliancy of their professional careers obscures the private character of the individual. They are seen through a misty veil and by their position shut out from the close observation of their fellows. It was my happiness to have known intimately, and to have enjoyed for many years the society of General Custer, and it may, therefore, be allowed me to record my impression of him as divested of the pomp of war, and mingling in the pursuits of social life. Abler hands may collect and engross the various incidents of this heroic life, compiling a suitable biography for his countrymen's instruction, and these reminiscences should be accepted simply as a tribute of affection to a dearly beloved friend. No one had followed General Custer's military career with more enthusiasm than the writer. The successive battles in which he bore so conspicuous and gallant a part were studied with ardor by his then unknown friend, who was thus prepared, should the moment ever arrive, to meet with interest and embrace with affection the hero whose deeds had already won ardent admiration. The stirring incidents of the war had developed two men whose exploits had made them objects of the writer's sincere attachment. Both young, their rapidity of promotion alike extraordinary and acquired by absolute merit, it was my happiness to claim their friendship and at last bring them together. In the war they had fought side by side, each unacquainted with the other, except in their achievements. At my fireside they came together in friendly meeting and cemented in private the attachment which sympathy of character always creates. One now lies ill among the Berkshire hills, his youthful form scarred with wounds received in his country's service; the other, dead at 37, sleeps where no stone may mark his resting-place, beneath the blood-stained sod of the cold and cheerless plains.

In the fall of 1866, while fulfilling an engagement at St. Louis, I met the General for the first time, and under such peculiar circumstances that they may bear narration. The play was over, the curtain fallen, and while still preparing to return to my hotel after my night's entertainment, a knock was heard at my dressing-room door. Obedient to the answering summons, entered a tall, fair-haired, blue-eyed, smiling gentleman, clad in military dress. Apologizing for the intrusion, he gave his name as General Custer. No such introduction was necessary. By those well-known features I recognized at once the young cavalry leader. He had been sent to bring me to the hotel where he was temporarily residing, while en route to his command at Fort Leavenworth. I was to go with him to meet Mrs. Custer and other members of his party. Excuses were set aside. He pleaded "orders" which must be obeyed, and refusal was impossible. A happy hour in his society was passed; and thus began an acquaintance, ripening within the next ten years into the most genuine friendship, in which I learned to esteem the qualities of the man as sincerely as I had admired the achievements of the soldier.

At that early time General Custer had not outgrown the habits of the camp. He still wore the long hair which is so familiar in his early pictures, his face was bronzed and sunburned by outdoor exposure, his bearing a mixture of the student and the soldier. No pen portrait of General Custer would be complete which did not give the simple, boyish side of his character, seemingly more marked from the daring, adventurous spirit which the war had made us familiar with. His voice was earnest, soft, tender and appealing, with a quickness of the utterance which became at times choked by the rapid flow of ideas, and a nervous hesitancy of speech, betraying intensity of thought. There was a searching expression of the eye which riveted the speaker, as if each word was being measured mercilessly by the listener. Peculiarly nervous, he yet seemed able to control himself at will. His fund of humor was betrayed by a chuckle of a laugh, such as those who have ever known Artemus Ward will remember—a laugh which became infectious and seemed to gurgle up from the depths of the full and joyous heart of the sunny, affectionate Custer.

In the years which passed on, following our first meeting, duty separated, vacations reunited us. Custer's appointment to duty in Kentucky afforded me several weeks of his society, during which we were rarely apart. At that time he ran over his remembrances of the war to me, speaking of himself with modesty, of others with enthusiasm, until it became a delight to listen. Thus I had the description of the winter campaign against the Indians on the Washita before it was in print, told in his graphic, fervent style, and acted over until it seemed as if I were a participant in the strife. At this time he began those sketches in the Galaxy which were at once received with favor. Again separated, we were next to meet during the tour of the Grand Duke Alexis, in whose suite he had been placed by the government. Here his truly American characteristics gained him a friend, whose quick eye discerned the depths of that genuine nature and valued it. The friendship which arose between the Russian Grand Duke and General Custer, from their association on this tour, was very honorable to both. The polished courtier discerned in the young Democrat those sterling qualities of manhood which maintained their individuality in the midst of ceremonies and flatteries, and the correspondence which passed between them upon the return of the Grand Duke to Russia was highly gratifying to Custer. Enjoying his vacation as keenly as a schoolboy, General Custer was always apparently "awaiting orders," and when they came, his whole manner changed; he seemed to put on the soldier with the uniform. He often said that his duties on the plains were the happiest events of his life—not that he loved war for war's sake, but that he loved to feel that he was on "duty." The freedom of the plains, the constant companionship of his idolized wife— now sitting in the shadow of her last and greatest bereavement— his horses and his gun, his regiment and its beloved officers, amply replaced the allurements of civil life.

It was impossible for Custer to appear otherwise than himself. He had none of that affectation of manner or bearing which arises from egotism or timidity. Reticent among strangers, even to a fault, his enemies, if he had any, must have recognized his perfect integrity of character. Indeed, this reticence often caused him to be misunderstood, and he himself frequently complained that he could not be "all things to all men." It was only in the companionship of his intimates and close friends that the real joyousness of his nature shone forth. Then he was all confidence, his eye would brighten, his face light up and his whole heart seemed to expand. He had something of the Frenchman in his gayety, much of the German in a certain tenacity of purpose. Utterly fearless of danger, he seemed in private to become as gentle as a woman.

(Some have thought that Custer's courage was of the bull-dog kind; that he knew no danger and feared none. Nothing can be further from the truth. He said to the writer that, the first few battles he was in, he was almost overcome with fear; he also intimates this very clearly in his "War Memoirs." His courage was purely a triumph of mind over physical fear. Toward the close of the war he became convinced that he would not be killed. The truth doubtless is that he was fully conscious that he possessed the ability to rise in his profession, and he had determined to do so at all hazards. He chose the post of danger at the head of his column simply because he was aware that it was the place to obtain success. He knew that thus, and thus only, he could inspire his men with confidence, and make of each a hero. All this was the result of a deliberate plan. He had counted the cost of success and was fully prepared to pay it. He wanted honor and distinction among his fellow-men, or death on the field. He put this spirit into his division by his example, and they were invincible.)*

In the society of ladies, with whom his deeds had made him a favorite, he manifested none of the gallantries which arise from vanity.

When ordered to Fort Lincoln, General Custer was lost to me for several months, but our correspondence was constant. He was eager that I should visit him, and it was only by a pressure of professional duties at the time that I was denied the pleasure of being his companion upon the first expedition to the Black Hills. The succeeding fall he made his vacation with me, and for two happy weeks we were constantly together. This was in Chicago. If an engagement to dinner took him away, he would hasten at its conclusion to my dress-room at the theater; and thence, arm-in-arm, we would return home together. Thus I have seen him in the midst of social temptations, sufficient to overcome ordinary men, maintain the strict sobriety of his habits. He never touched wine, nor used tobacco in any form, and I never heard a profane word from his lips. His obstinate valor as a soldier made him courteous and forgiving to a defeated enemy and he became a Democrat in his opinions, regarding the manner in which the

---

* Remarks by another intimate friend of General Custer.

South should be treated after the close of the rebellion. This made him unpopular at headquarters, and perhaps influenced his promotion and hindered his career. He loved his profession and was jealous of its fame, tenacious of the honor of his cloth, and intolerant of the abuses which the army suffered by that pernicious system wherein politics were the means by which many unworthy men entered the service. He had that love of military display which distinguishes the Frenchman, and his uniform was the badge of his glory. A fondness for theatrical representations he shared in common with the members of his profession, and a more enthusiastic auditor I never saw.

The last winter of Custer's life now approaches. He had obtained leave of absence for two months, intending to spend his time in New York; and, that he might leave behind him a record of his career, and also that he might eke out his slender income, his sketches in the Galaxy were resumed. It was during this vacation, extended to five months in all, that the happiest hours of my association with him were passed. Being myself for the winter in New York, we made all our engagements mutual, going into company together, meeting at my own fireside always on Sundays; and each evening during the run of "Julius Caesar," the place of honor in my dressing-room at Booth's was filled by my dear friend. Those were indeed happy hours. I recall especially one passed at the Century Club, where he was the recipient of great attentions. How bright and joyous he was, and how eager that his friend should know and enjoy the friendship of those whom he himself esteemed. Surrounded by the followers of literature, sicence, and art, and their cultured patrons, the young soldier, whose whole life and education were of the camp, attracted the attention and won the respect of all who met him. With that rare facility given but to few, he drew from the artist and the historian the best fruits of their labors, and as warmly listened as he could warmly speak. His love for art was no affected dilettantism. Appreciating the glories of nature with an enthusiast's soul, he learned to trace her likeness in the works of her copyists. The studio of Bierstadt was a happy resting-place for him. Here, while the great painter labored, the young soldier would lovingly follow the master hand, identifying the exactness of the picture by his own knowledge of the scenery or groupings so vividly reproduced. It has been said that "military experience so exhausts the body, by daily, and for the most part useless exercises, that it renders it difficult to cultivate one's mind," but this was not true of General Custer. Not having received in his youth the advantages of a college education, he betrayed the keenest desire for knowledge and cultivation.

(General Custer was a great reader, and his taste ran almost entirely in the line of the best literature. His pleasure seemed to be to constantly add to his stock of information. He spent a large share of his time during the winter seasons in reading such works as "Napier's Peninsular War," "Napoleon's Campaigns," and works of this class, which would perfect him in his profession. Often he would spend a whole day and a large part of the night over a few pages of these works: having a large map before him, he was determined to fully understand each movement and campaign made by these great masters of the art of war. Perfection in his chosen profession seemed to be the mainspring of all his actions. He was ready to make any and all sacrifices which would contribute to this end. He seemed thoroughly to have adopted the motto that "nothing is done while anything remains to be accomplished." His powers of mental work were fully equal to his physical endurance; six hours of sleep seemed to be all he required, and his great mental activity rendered it almost impossible for him to be idle an hour.)

A distinguished gentleman whose Friday evenings at his home on Fifth Avenue were regarded as happy privileges for the best minds of the metropolis, extended to the General hospitality and advantages which were eagerly accepted and as earnestly enjoyed. Here where the flame of thought was of the loftiest character, Custer would sit, an attentive and admiring listener, drinking from the rich fountain of instruction. After an evening thus passed, and upon emerging into the silent avenue, the impressions of the recent conversation still upon us, excited by the interchange of friendly converse, he would take my arm, and against my entreaty become my escort home, alleging as a reason his want of exercise, although I knew that in his loving care he feared some danger might befall his friend, and thus went far out of his way to see me safely housed. Such acts as these, trivial though they seem in narration, are those which make that fearful day in June so terrible to me, making it seem impossible that I am never again to clasp that hand so true and tried, never again to look into that face so dearly loved.

The winter passed only too quickly. His original leave of two months had been granted by his immediate superior, General Terry, his friend as well as commander, and his extended leave came from General Sheridan, no less friendly. But another extension, earned by him surely through his months of labor at Fort Lincoln, was refused as soon as asked, and he was at once ordered to rejoin his regiment by General Belknap, then Secretary of War. For some unexplained reason, General Custer believed the Secretary to be his enemy, and dreaded the final appeal for that extension of leave which his affairs so much demanded. When refusal came, although it disappointed him, it did not the less find him prepared for obedience to orders. His literary work for the Galaxy had been undertaken, as has been stated, to eke out his income and more generously support the expenses of his family, and he had formed another plan by which he hoped to still more liberally provide for the future of all those dependent upon him. The agent of the Literary Bureau, Mr. Redpath, of Boston, having made him a liberal offer to deliver a number of lectures during the next winter, he was, at the moment the Secretary's orders came, perfecting his plans to that end. After the summer's campaign he was again to visit New York, his lecture in the meantime to be written, and we were to "rehearse" his appearance before the public passed judgment upon him. This project was left incomplete as to details, but he looked forward to its accomplishment as a happy means of increasing his income and meeting face to face his admirers, the public.

Custer went one March day upon his journey. No forebodings of evil embittered the parting; we were to meet again. He had not yet fallen under the public accusation which was afterwards hurled upon him. Although he left so many pleasant associations and gave up so many personal enjoyments, he was going to his duty, and that sufficed. A winter trip across the Dakota plains had no terrors for him, nor for her who never left his side while it was her privilege to remain there. After many hardships they at last reached Fort Lincoln, and then began his preparations for the fatal expedition. Loving friends, unacquainted with the details of warfare, and jealous only of his reputation, will always, perhaps unjustly, believe that had all gone forward as it began, under his own personal control, the disaster and annihilation which followed would never have occurred. No reflection upon the capacity of General Custer's superiors is here intended, but it may be justly claimed that the complications which followed as the result of the appearance before the investigating committee at Washington arose, in a great measure, from the disorders of a change of command almost in the enemy's front; that suspicion on the one side and crippled powers, laboring under ungenerous and undeserved imputations, upon the other, created a confusion which could not but be detrimental. The belief will always prevail among the friends of General Custer that familiarity with the Indian mode of warfare, a certain subtlety in his preparations for attack or resistance, and the "dash" which has never been denied him, well fitted him to organize and conduct such a campaign. He who had so often challenged the bravest of the red warriors and wrung from them the title of the "Big Yellow Chief," was fully able not only to lead his own "gallant Seventh," but also to organize the campaign and overlook the plan. This was denied him. At the supreme moment of his fortunes he was summoned to Washington.

CHAPTER XII

Crook's column was on the headwaters of the Tongue River on the 7th of June and on the 8th a war party came down un-expectedly and tried to stampede the cavalry horses, which was repulsed while bringing on a skirmish. Now Crook seemed to be perfectly satisfied with this repulse instead of pursuing and cap-turing every man, dead or alive. There could not have been more than one hundred of them, and there were fresh men and fresh horses that had no endurance, only the march that could have been commanded to pursue and capture every man, dead or alive. These Indians, in my opinion, just did what they wanted, and that was to find out the strength of Crook's column, which was a clever move on their part. Instead of being pursued, they were let go, which was a great mistake and did not look well for a commencement.

He ought to have had his outpost out so as to give warning for this assault on his troops, but there was nothing, although he was seeking the enemy.

Now on the 17th of June there was another blunder, one which was disastrous and was caught even unsaddled when the scouts came in and gave the alarm. He formed a line with the infantry and they advanced to meet the Indians, who attacked and fought desperately. On the left were bluffs which they thought was a good cover, but finding out later was to their disadvantage.

Captain Nickerson perceived a fault in the line and advanced himself and made a kind of a left wheel, so as to get them out of the position they were in, but it was too late; the Indians charged and blocked the flank and there was heavy work by our infantry and allied Indians which caused a great deal of confusion.

This ended my services in the expedition. My arm, where I was shot was useless and therefore I was sent down with the wounded to Fort Laramie. We got there on the 25th of June, stayed there a day and then went to Cheyenne and then to Fort Russell, where I settled up my affairs and then to Mr. Chas. Kimber, where I roomed before I went. Upon my arrival at Kimber's I found everything as I had left it.

Before leaving with the expedition I had given Mr. Kimbers a letter which he was not to open until he had heard from me or had heard that I was knocked out. Everything settled up, the next day I left for San Francisco and arrived there in time for the Fourth of July.

While watching the Fourth of July parade of magnificency, with their gay uniforms and banners outspread, which was to commemorate the day of freedom that our forefathers had fought for, we were enjoying it; but then, think of those poor Indians who had done no crime only fighting for freedom, that I had just been fighting against.

As I know no more what transpired with these columns after the Rosebud River engagement, I did my best endeavors to procure all information up to the last battle, as I know the reader wants to know from start to finish of this important expedition.

CHAPTER XIII

When I was in San Francisco, 1876, I met a builder named Harrison. We became partners in the contracting and building business. His son, Fred Harrison, lives here in Honolulu. I became acquainted with a contractor named Thomas. He and I decided to go to Australia. Our boat stopped at Honolulu for part of the day. We walked up to the Pali to take a look at the country. A French Canadian was digging a well. The clay from the well looked to us like mighty good pottery clay. We tossed up a silver dollar, heads to stay in Honolulu and start a brickyard and pottery works, tails to go to Australia. Heads came up. This was in 1877. We went to the minister of the interior and I said to him, "We want to lease twenty acres up at the Pali. We want to start a brickyard." He said, "If you will make bricks, I will give you a deed to fifty acres." We found that the clay had too much vegetable matter and volcanic matter in it and the bricks cracked so we had to give it up. We decided to go on to Australia, but C. R. Bishop, the banker, advised us to stay here, as King Kalakaua had signed a treaty of reciprocity with the United States, which meant there would be several sugar mills built here. This proved to be the case, and we had all we could do.

I was married fifty years ago to Kaumaka Cummins, the eldest daughter of John A. Cummins, for whom the Cummins School is named. We have three children, Cummins Walker, John S. Walker and Matilda Walker. Our son John is consulting engineer at San Francisco. During the fifty years or more I have lived here I have installed sugar machinery in Australia, the Fijis and at various places on the islands here, including the Philippines.

CHAPTER XIV

My Part in the Revolution of 1895

Mr. Samuel Nowlein had talked to me about the opinion of several citizens and a majority of the natives who were willing to have the Hawaiian Islands annexed to the United States and not for protectorate. He asked me what I thought about it, and I told him that I thought an annexation right out by the United States would be far better.

I received all of my orders from Samuel Nowlein. "Well," I said, "we have no arms and ammunition." He said that would be all right, for there will be all that we want from San Francisco; that the financier was on his way there with a man that knew his business who was going to transact this for arms and ammunition. "Well," I said, "have you spoken to the natives about it, and what forces have you that you could depend on?" He said he had and found no trouble in getting them. They seemed to be all anxious for a turn in the government from what it was at the present time. I sanctioned that I would help. "What do you want me to do?" He asked me how many men I thought I could get. That I couldn't say for the present. I knew quite a few white men as well as natives whom I thought would be quite willing to help under the circumstances.

Samuel Nowlein said that he would like to have me take the Police Station, as it was the talk that there would be several men there from the Boston as well as other white men. I said all right, although I knew my forces were small for such a job.

I got Mr. Bertelmann to make some cores for the casting of hand grenades. The core is used to form the inside of the hand grenade, which is metal. These hand grenades were made with just a quarter of an inch hole, so that I could get my dynamite and buck shot in and insert a fuse with a percussion cap. These fuses were just long enough for fifteen seconds and would explode at that time when thrown or bowled against the enemy. These hand grenades, when filled with slugs, buckshot and dynamite, were very destructive. These hand grenades were different from the regulation type of the service, which were used by the army and navy. The service hand grenades had wooden plugs inserted which bore the time of these fuses. These hand grenades of the service could not be bowled along the ground, but mine you could, because there was only the fuse; that would give me a great advantage. I could bowl them at any advancing enemy, especially in formation of platoons or company, and the explosion among them would give my men a great advantage.

T. B. WALKER AND MAJOR STUART

Mr. Samuel Nowlein, on the first of January, 1895, told me the arms and ammunition would be in at the old fish market wharf at 10 o'clock at night on a Thursday evening, January 3rd. I went around and warned my lieutenants of this fact. I had then some three hundred and fifty men, about forty of them white men, the rest natives and half-whites.

I went to Mr. John Colburn's hay and feed store, at the bottom of Nuuanu street, and found that he had a great many bales of hay which would be very handy for barricades, if necessary.

I then acquainted my lieutenants and men of these facts; they were to assemble not later than 9 o'clock on the evening of the 3rd. Previous to this I had given Mr. Samuel Nowlein one dozen of these hand grenades and three to Mr. John Bowler to wreck the telephone structure where all the wires were connected, which was then located on Merchant street. I showed him how to use these hand grenades. I made him practice with the fifteen-second fuse. He said, "All right, I understand it now." This was at my house. I walked with him as far as King street, where the mule cars came in from Waikiki. He got on the car that Joe Fern was driving. Joe Fern afterwards became Mayor of Oahu. I happened to get on the same car the next morning and Joe Fern told me that he had these three hand grenades that I gave Bowler. He said Bowler was not on the car five minutes before he almost fainted. Joe Fern asked Bowler what was the matter and Bowler replied, "Here, take these," and Joe Fern took the three hand grenades. I said, "What have you done with them?" Joe Fern replied that he had put them where nobody would ever get them. Joe had nothing to do with this thing and was asked not to say anything about it, and he didn't.

CHAPTER XV

On the 3rd, at 8 o'clock in the evening, I prepared to go down. I had one dozen hand grenades, four revolvers and ammunition for them. It was heavy and rather awkward to carry. My wife said, "Tom, let me drive you down," as she was game enough to volunteer. "Well, all right, dear." I then harnessed up the horse and we started off, turning up Punahou street and then on to Beretania street, and went straight down until we got to Alakea street. I then went about one hundred yards from the Y. M. C. A. and said, "My dear, you had better get out from here; there seems to be no one about." I kissed her and bid her good-night. I went straight down to the waterfront until I got to Queen street. I then turned towards the old fish market, where my men were to assemble. My men started coming in about eight-thirty. My men were very slow until a few more came up, which amounted to two hundred and twenty-seven men, including forty white men.

We waited anxiously for the boat that Nowlein said would be in at 10 o'clock. At twenty minutes to one a native came in on horseback with a note from Nowlein, stating that the boat would not be in, that they had to run ashore by Diamond Head and bury everything in the sand; to disperse my men until I heard from him the next day. I did not see him the next day, but on Saturday morning I did see him. He said that my men would get all the arms they needed. These arms were brought from Waikiki close to where Antone Rosa's cottage was and distributed to my men.

I did not have enough arms and ammunition, but I had rifles which really belonged to the men in my battalion, and they had ammunition, so it was no use of making a complaint. Time was too short for that, so I thought I would make the best of it, saying nothing of it. Nowlein told me that I would hear from him on Sunday night between 8 and 9 o'clock, telling me what time the main attack would take place and that I would have lots of assistance from the forces. With that I had simply to notify my lieutenants and men. On the Sunday night about eight-thirty two of my lieutenants came to my house and told me what had happened out at the Bertelmann house—Mr. Carter was shot and that large forces were getting out there with the government. I said, "Boys, it's all off; go right into town again and advise all you see to go and volunteer to join the government forces; those who do not want to may go to work as usual in the morning." I had ended my part in the revolution.

About a week after this I was painting my front gate when a sergeant with four men of the government forces appeared and said, "Walker, I want you." I said, "What is the matter?" "Well, we want you." I said, "Wait a while until I clean up." These four men came down with a charge and I flung the muzzles up with my hands and said, "What is the matter with you fellows? I have nothing here but a paint brush in my hand." They were so nervous even when I threw their rifles up that they did not resist. Just then I saw a man coming up towards us. A little closer it turned out to be Mr. Dillingham. He came up and said, "What's the matter, Tom?" "Well, I guess you know all about it. Mr. Dillingham, I'll go with you peaceably; you can send these fellows away; I just want to go in the house and have a shave and clean up and I'll go with you if you will wait." He said that was all right and came in the yard and sat on the veranda talking to my wife and children. My wife was well acquainted with Mr. Dillingham.

When I had finished cleaning up I went with him. Two or three days passed and then they began to give me cross-examinations, and lots of it, and then I was sent over to the Oahu prison. In about four days Arthur Brown came over to the prison; it was then about 10 o'clock at night. The police came to my cell and said, "Dress; you are wanted; the sheriff is here for you." I saw that it was Arthur Brown. He said, "I want you to come over to the Station House, Walker." When we arrived at the Police Station I was put in the cell and half an hour afterwards I was taken upstairs to a room where the judge advocates and holds more of the offices. Mr. Thurston, Mr. W. O. Smith, Mr. Kinney and one or two others did the principal questioning.

Mr. W. O. Smith asked me if I knew anything about these bombs which they had on the table stacked up like you might have seen cannon balls stacked in front of a barrack gate or arsenal. I said, "Yes, I know all about them; I had them made." "What did you have them made for?" "I had them made to bowl or throw at the enemy whenever I might come in contact with them." "What's inside of them?" he asked. I replied, "buckshot." "Then you acknowledge the fact that you had them made? You are guilty of that?" "Yes, I am guilty." Now there were several questions asked about other citizens, some of them well-to-do, but I knew nothing, and that was all they could get out of me. I was guilty and that was all. I never gave a man away. I preferred death before dishonor under these circumstances.

CHAPTER XVI

The trial came on. I was sentenced to serve thirty-five years, with a fine of two thousand dollars.

About two days after the trial one of the guards, who was acting as sentry on the upper part of the prison, dropped a little note in the prison yard where I was allowed to walk for a little while. The note read, "Gulick, Rickard, Steward and yourself: the mob outside wants to lynch you or have you hanged." In the afternoon I was taken to the cell, which made me think there was some truth in it. Three or four days after that the American Consul came over and asked to see me. I was called up and went into a room. The American Consul was there. Mr. Low talked with the Consul and the Consul told him to please leave the room and then began to question me. He said he had heard that I had fought under the American flag. I said, "Yes, I was with Reynolds in the engagement of Powder River against Crazy Horse, where I was wounded in the neck. The wounded, including myself, were sent in from Lodge Pole to Fort Phil Kearney. On June 7, 1876, I was with General Crook at the Rosebud River when attacked by Sitting Bull." I was also wounded in the Rosebud River engagement and showed the Consul my wounds. I told him I was not enrolled in the army, but had volunteered to go as a rigger, knotting and splicing. I was taken on at Fort Russell, about three miles across the prairie from Cheyenne. He asked me how I came to go to Cheyenne. I told him that a man had come on the train and asked if there were any bricklayers on board and I said yes, I am a bricklayer, and he said there's a couple of months' work here at six dollars a day. The Consul said "That is what I want to know." Well, I said I had my ticket from New York to San Francisco and told this contractor of the fact that my trunk had gone ahead. He said he would sell my ticket for me and get my trunk back, so I was not much the loser.

I told the Consul from then on I went to work for this man. In about six weeks the work was finished and there was talk about an expedition that was going to be sent after the Indians. I was then acquainted with Mr. Hickok, "Wild Bill," as he was called. Mr. Hickok was a scout at the time of the Northern and Southern war. He was a great friend of Captain Tom Custer. He told me that in the letter Tom Custer had said that there might be trouble with the Indians later on. After finishing up the job I was on, I went to Dakota and there I talked with Captain Tom Custer and his two brothers, George and Boston Custer. I had the letter of introduction from Mr. Hickok. Mr. Custer said he was forage master of the Seventh Cavalry and that he would need assistance if the expedition went. I gave him my address and he said he would let me know when he knew for sure. I went back and went to work again on another job. Then Mr. Hickok heard that Custer had to go to Washington as witness because of wrong doings with graft in regard to the horse feed. Of course, that spoiled my plans concerning my promise from Boston Custer. I heard that they were taking on a few drivers at Fort Russell. I was asked if I was an American citizen. I said "No, I have been in the country only four months." I told him that I was a good rigger, knotting and splicing. He said, "See me in the morning." I did see him and was taken on. That is how I came to stop in Cheyenne. Now I have stated the way I happen to be in Cheyenne. He said, "Well, Mr. Walker, they talk about hanging, but I don't think there will be any hanging." He shook hands with me and bid me good-day. Things quieted down very much after this. It was almost a month when Mr. Low received plans for the building of dark cells from the mainland. He sent for me to come up to the office and gave me the roll of plans and said, "Look these over and see if you understand them all." I looked over these and said I perfectly understood them, and he asked me if I was confident that I could do them. "That I am sure of," I said. "They are very simple." In about two weeks we started to build the cells. I was the only bricklayer. Of course, I had to make bricklayers out of the prisoners there who were in for the same crime as I was. Mr. Carl Widemann and Mr. Wm. Greig, myself and others started the work along all right. We got a little better diet than the ordinary prison fare and were let out a little longer at night instead of the time the other prisoners were allowed. We finished the work satisfactorily, so they had a brand-new set of dark cells with a current of air running through each cell, but still no windows, pitch dark. After this was finished I was let go in the carpenter shop to do a little work there, such as being sent to repair some drains that got stopped up, and other things necessary about the prison. Mr. Low had told me that I might get out sooner than I had expected, as he heard very good reports from the prison committee.

On the 28th of November, 1895, Mr. Rickard and myself were let go. When I got out I went and thanked Mr. Dole and the ministry for being pardoned. They all spoke freely and very nicely to me. I then started to follow my profession, as usual, the building trade.

When Bertelmann and Nowlein were arrested they turned state's evidence and even gave the authorities the hand grenades which I had made for the use that I have formerly mentioned. I thought it very low and mean of them, but then I couldn't say anything.

My wife deserves credit for taking me down on the Thursday night. It showed her bravery, knowing the consequences, as I had told her, if anybody offers to arrest me with these things on my person I have got to shoot them and make the best of my way down to my men, because being arrested with these destructive weapons on my person is a very serious crime. But it so happened that there wasn't any one in my pathway. I had a clear course right down to where I was to meet my men.

Had I received a note from Nowlein on the Sunday evening and knowing that he was so far out from his base of attack, I don't believe that I would have attacked, because I would have had no show with my small body of men, knowing well that at this time the government was aware of these men being out near

Diamond Head. This information concerning the government being aware of these men out near Diamond Head I received by one of my lieutenants, who in turn received the same information from one of his friends who had been walking along the beach and had seen Nowlein's men. I knew that Nowlein would not get in to be of any support to me because all the roads would have been blocked and I would have had to play a lone hand and that meant keeping the last cartridge for myself.

It seems to me there is always some sacrifice to be made in these uprisings, and it seems that Mr. Carter was the sacrifice.

Had I started anything in the town it would have been a very serious affair, for I would have to carry it through as far as my limits went in regard to ammunitions. Having been annexed later on by the United States, I thank God that these serious things did not happen, for it would have been serious for more than one family. I have nothing to say about any one else, because it would be useless, but I do regret to think that these two men, namely, Nowlein and Bertelmann, acted the curs they did in not caring who sunk as long as they swam.